THE SCHOLAR-LIBRARIAN

Books, Libraries, and the Visual Arts

The

SCHOLAR-
LIBRARIAN

*Books, Libraries, and the
Visual Arts*

RICHARD WENDORF

The Boston Athenæum and Oak Knoll Press 2005

First Edition, published in 2005 by

Oak Knoll Press
310 Delaware Street, New Castle, DE 19720 USA
Web: http://www.oakknoll.com

and

The Boston Athenæum
10½ Beacon Street
Boston, Massachusetts 02108

ISBN: 1-58456-159-9 (Oak Knoll Press)

Title: The Scholar-Librarian
Author: Richard Wendorf
Typographer: Scott J. Vile
Dustjacket Design: Scott J. Vile
Publishing Director: J. Lewis von Hoelle

This work was printed and bound in the United States of America on archival, acid-free paper meeting the requirements of the American Standard for Permanence of Paper for Printed Library Materials.

for Terry Belanger

Contents

Preface

T HE TEN ESSAYS collected in this volume are devoted
to subjects that are central to my life as a scholar and as
a library director. Books, libraries, and the fine arts have
been the focus of my work for the past thirty years: first as a
teacher of English literature and art history at Northwestern
University, then as a librarian and art historian at Harvard, and
most recently as the director of a library that is also, in many
ways, still a museum. I am delighted that essays on each of these
subjects could be bound together within the covers of this one
book.

My career has not been a straightforward one, nor has it
been carefully premeditated. As a scholar as well as an administrator, I have followed various twists in the road when my
curiosity was piqued and the timing seemed right. I was
trained to teach and write about English and American literature, and I decided, fairly early in my education, to focus on the
"long" eighteenth century in England, with a particular
emphasis on poetry and biographical narrative. I essentially
backed into art history because of my interest in comparing
eighteenth-century biography with contemporary portrait-
painting. This turned out to be an ambitious and sometimes
unwieldy project that led in many directions: to a scholarly
book, of course; to an ongoing exploration of the relationships
between literature and the visual arts; and eventually to a

1

teaching appointment (at Harvard) in the Fine Arts rather than the English department. That was an odd moment indeed, for I was beginning my career as a library director at the same time, fully aware that I now had two jobs neither of which I had been trained to pursue. This may have been a brave decision on my part — or sheer foolhardiness, as I now tend to believe — but in the long run I have no reason to regret the directions I have taken, especially since books (both as texts and as physical objects) remain such an important part of my life as a scholar as well as an administrator.

Four of the following essays (the first three and the penultimate, "The Secret Life of Type") have been written expressly for this collection. Two of the remaining essays are also recent — "Piranesi's Double Ruin" and "Abandoning the Capital" — and have been reprinted here in part because of the close relation they bear to two of the new essays ("Living with Piranesi" and "The Secret Life of Type"). The other four chapters, on critical and bibliographical subjects, have been chosen from among two dozen or so previously published essays, some of which have been expanded and reprinted in my monographs, and some of which simply don't strike me, for a variety of reasons, as being eminently collectable. I have therefore been selective, preferring to shepherd a few essays comfortably back into print rather than presenting my readers with an indigestible bill of fare. I should add, moreover, that readers familiar with my work may be surprised that I have not included essays on British art in this volume. You will find the most recent of these writings collected in *After Sir Joshua: Essays on British Art and Cultural History*, published by Yale University Press for the Paul Mellon Centre for Studies in British Art in 2005.

I have divided the ten chapters in this book into three sections. The first three essays are devoted to libraries and to collecting, and they have been written from a personal as well as a professional point of view. The second three chapters are critical pieces that address three different media: poetry, etching, and film. The final four essays focus on bibliography, typography, and the history of the book. These are naturally somewhat arbitrary distinctions, however, and the perceptive reader will discover in the critical and typographical essays how central the subjects of medium and materiality are to my engagement with texts of all kinds.

It gives me pleasure to disburse a number of debts that I have incurred during the preparation of this volume. I am grateful to the trustees of the Boston Athenæum for supporting the production of this book, for supporting my scholarly research, and for supporting the work of many scholar-librarians. Robert Fleck and John von Hoelle of Oak Knoll Press have been collegial and encouraging collaborators, and Scott Vile of the Ascensius Press has once again provided me with his expert skills as a designer and typographer. My colleagues at the Athenæum continue to provide the professional environment that is conducive to writing essays such as these. Special thanks go to my executive secretary, Catherine Cooper, and to Ann Wadsworth, our editor of publications, who have worked closely with me on this experiment in resuscitation.

I also wish to thank a number of friends and colleagues who have wrestled with one or more of the four new essays in this volume: Terry Belanger, David Dearinger, Lori Anne Ferrell, Elizabeth Lyman, Marshall Moriarty, Leslie Morris, Elizabeth Morse, Carol Rothkopf, Charles Ryskamp, Patricia Meyer Spacks, Roger Stoddard, James Wendorf, and John Wilton-Ely. I am indebted to the journals and presses that have granted us permission to reprint the earlier essays in this book; I cite each press or journal in the "tailnote" to various chapters. I have made a few minor corrections in these earlier essays — and have set the footnotes in a more consistent style — but the texts otherwise appear in their original form.

Part One

Chapter 1
The Petrified Mouse

I N THE SUMMER OF 1989, just a few weeks before I was to forsake Chicago for the banks of the Charles, my friends Helen and Michael Goodkin hosted a small but festive party on my behalf. I had been a professor and a dean, and I was soon to become a library director; wasn't it about time I met some proper librarians, they kindly asked? I found one of their guests to be particularly interesting, as virtually everyone did when meeting Robert Rosenthal for the first time. He was the legendary proprietor of the special collections department at the University of Chicago, someone who ran his shop the old-fashioned way — and ran it well. Serving an apprenticeship with him was a much-coveted experience, for Bob possessed a marvelous sense of humor as well as a profound knowledge of

I delivered "The Petrified Mouse: Reflections on My First Two Years at the Houghton Library" to participants in Rare Book School at Columbia University in July 1991. That initial lecture was subsequently reprised and expanded for a number of audiences, eventually under the title "A Tale of Two Libraries." None of these lectures was ever written down as a formal script, and both the master tape and my own tape of the original talk at Columbia are blank, as it turns out. I have therefore based this essay on my notes for those lectures and have cast it, appropriately, in the past tense. It is published here for the first time.

rare books and manuscripts. I learned, for example, that he had formed a tontine to collect books published in the year 1900. According to Terry Belanger, the "three members of the group were Michael Turner (then head of special collections at the Bodleian), Rosenthal, and myself," but only Rosenthal took the project seriously, discovering a cheap copy of the *Cumulative Book Index* for 1900 virtually the day after the trio first made their unusual compact.*

Near the end of the evening, Bob took me aside and confided that he had a small anecdote to share with me, something that I might find useful once I had made my way to the Houghton Library. It was actually an academic joke, one that he had probably heard many years ago. Here's how it goes:

There once was a man who had two sons — identical twins — whom he simply couldn't tell apart. When they turned eighteen, he therefore decided to send one to New Haven to become a rowdy and the other to Cambridge to become a gentleman. True to form, one son became a Yale rowdy and the other a Harvard gentleman, but when they returned to their father following their graduation, he still couldn't tell them apart.

In the following seven and a half years (and even longer, I must confess) I told this joke many times and always to good effect.

---

* Here's more of the story from Belanger: "We were sitting around in the early or mid 1980s, thinking, we're so smart, what should we be collecting that will be worth money someday, but are cheap now. Books published in 1900, we decided, working toward a great exhibition to be opened in London (Earl's Court, we thought) in the year 2000 by Mrs. Elizabeth Turner, assisted by the Queen, and in New York (perhaps in a special building in Central Park) by Mrs. Jane Rosenthal. Neither Michael Turner nor I thought that we were serious — but Rosenthal did."

No one seems to have heard it before, everyone finds it amusing, and everyone appears to find it amusing in his or her own particular way. For some, the point is that a rowdy at Yale is essentially the same thing as a gentleman at Harvard. For others, the joke affirms what many believe but rarely admit, which is that august institutions such as Yale and Harvard don't really have that much influence on the young men and women who enter their gates. For still others, the moral is even more general, which is that certain gentlemen are in fact rowdy and that certain men who try to be rowdy are — no matter how hard they try — still very much gentlemen. Each time I finish this joke, there is a slight interval (perhaps only the proverbial nanosecond) before the first ripple of laughter begins, and then a continuing rumble of approval as the intricacy of the tale finally takes hold.

During my career as a library director at Harvard, I drew upon this amusing fable both to break the ice at the beginning of a talk and, more importantly, to remind those who view the world through crimson-colored glasses that the university (and its libraries) are not in fact unique: older, larger, and richer perhaps, but not unlike other American institutions in a number of important ways. Space restrictions, the preservation and conservation of collections, the challenges and promises of technology, changing patterns in scholarship, limited resources, greater visibility (and perceived accessibility) within the larger community — all of these are important and often pressing issues that confront every research library in America, and Harvard is no exception. The oldest, largest, and richest university library in this country might even be thought of as the progenitor of many of its competitors, the model from which the blueprint for academic library systems has been so successfully (and expensively) implemented. Without Houghton, for instance, there would arguably be no rowdy Beinecke at Yale, let alone an even rowdier Ransom Humanities Center in Texas, both of which are now richer (and perhaps larger) than their hard-scrabble cousin in Cambridge. The fundamental point I there-fore had the temerity to make, first at Harvard and then to sympathetic audiences outside the university, was that the Houghton Library had a good deal to learn from (as well as to contribute to) the wider library community.

At first glance it appeared to me, moreover, that "haughty" Houghton was showing its age. The climate-control system, which had been state-of-the-art when the library opened its doors in 1942, was very much in need of renovation in 1989. The books and manuscripts were cataloged in four different places in three different buildings, and there was no plan for a retro-spective conversion of the catalog cards to electronic form. The stacks were full and 40 percent of the manuscripts had not been cataloged. Planning had not begun on the library's fiftieth anniversary, which was to be celebrated in less than three years. When I tried to set up my computer in my new and rather grand office, I discovered that there were no three-pronged electrical outlets there. Later in the same day I discovered that my secretary, who had announced her departure a few weeks before I arrived, was the only staff member who had a computer for other than cataloging purposes; everyone else used a type-writer or wrote letters by hand.

I also learned that my new position was not necessarily a comfortable one in other respects. My immediate predecessor had been translated to Widener; *his* predecessor had taken early retirement, consoling himself by teaching bibliography courses in the English department. The recent chair of that department told me that his colleagues referred to Houghton as "the mau-soleum." The current chair of the English department told me that Houghton was essentially an obsolete institution; none of his professorial colleagues would darken our doors. The "archive," he kindly informed me, consisted not of books and manuscripts in special collections libraries, but of a handful of seminal theoretical texts, which varied from scholar to scholar. The college librarian (to whom I reported) confessed that she would not be able to make me the associate librarian for special collections, which she had promised to do when I was being recruited: "what would the heads of the other special libraries think?" The director of the university library was fond of saying, as a form of compliment, that "we threw Richard straight into the deep end, and he came right back to the surface." It was not an auspicious beginning.

It was not my life's ambition, as you can imagine, to dog-paddle in troubled waters, but it *was* important to examine the circumstances that produced such metaphors. I had never worked, or studied, or lived anywhere before where intelligent people actually explained that things were done in a certain manner "because they've always been done that way." One incident in particular will illustrate my predicament. Soon after I arrived at Houghton, a colleague came into my office late one afternoon to inform me that something serious had been discovered in the stacks. I asked what it was. "A mouse," I was told. Dead or alive, I asked? "Dead." Recently dead, I asked, or dead for some time? "Oh, dead for some time. It's petrified." I thanked my colleague for this information, but he did not leave. I asked what the matter was. "Is it all right to dispose of the mouse?" Of course, I answered; why did he ask? "Because nothing in the Houghton Library is to be discarded without the permission of the Librarian."

I was used to working in a university that looked forward and outward; I now found myself attempting to flourish in one that often seemed to look backward and inward. I was used to living in a city that, without ignoring its own extraordinary history, had its eye clearly focused on where it was headed. I now lived in a city that sometimes appeared to be obsessed with where it came from and often suspicious of changes that would alter that precious status quo. I was told again and again how pleased I must be to have moved from Chicago, usually by people whom I was fairly sure had never set foot there. Instead of answering them directly, I usually replied that Chicago was a metropolitan city, whereas Boston was cosmopolitan — a mischievous response that somehow seemed to get me off the hook.

It did not help, moreover, that Houghton was perceived as being not just special but somehow aloof: a mausoleum to the professoriate, perhaps, but an aristocratic establishment in the minds of many of our colleagues in Harvard's other libraries. Our senior cataloger, Hugh Amory, characterized these distinctions in architectural terms.

> Rare book libraries come in three varieties: the familiar temple, a form they share with public libraries; the corporate headquarters, specimens of which may be seen in the Beinecke Library or the Humanities Research Center in Austin; and the private house, as in the Morgan or the Huntington. At Harvard, Widener is the Parish Church, and Houghton is the Manor House. The social implications of this are not lost on our readers.

Nor, I should add, on one's fellow librarians — or on the general public, should anyone actually be tempted to visit us. It was one thing to point out that Houghton (unlike Widener) did not charge visiting scholars for access to its collections, but it was quite another thing to combat the general perception that the library was essentially an elitist institution. Comments like David Nyhan's in the *Boston Globe* didn't make matters any better. Writing on behalf of a beleaguered television program entitled "The 10 O'clock News," Nyhan confessed that "at times it could be so arch, so fey, so prissy, so unremittingly correct, you'd choke. It's like the Houghton Library at Harvard; not for everybody, sure, but it's damned important there is at least one of its kind hereabouts." With friends like these, one hardly needed enemies.

The challenge, of course, was to be "correct" — to be shrewd, wise, thoughtful, enterprising — without being either prissy or fey. But how to begin? An important first step consisted in persuading our colleagues at the university that we were a welcoming institution. Generations of undergraduates had been put off by the sight of this neo-Georgian manor house situated near the center of Harvard Yard; it was time to invite them in. We did so by encouraging faculty members in the humanities and social sciences to consider including Houghton's materials in their assignments, and even to teach their seminars within our walls. I offered to speak to each department; when I did, I discovered that there was genuine interest in putting our resources to work as well as considerable surprise that we were willing to reach out to constituencies that had long felt neglected. Within a relatively short time, certainly in less than two years, we were almost the victims of our own success as professors in various departments asked to hold their classes within the library. In order to emphasize our new role, we had the old wooden doors replaced by clear glass, which was the most dramatic physical gesture we could make in the direction of demystification and inclusiveness.

Just as important was our effort to work together with "the Wadsworths and the Wideners," as one of my associates referred to the university and college librarians. My colleagues and I took on more committee assignments, served on more search committees, and joined the queue to implement a strategic planning process deep in the bowels of haughty Houghton; I agreed to run the Fine Arts Library for almost a year. In return, we were included in Harvard's massive retrospective conversion project as well as in the planning and use of the new depository library system — the much-emulated "HD." Once our fiftieth anniversary was upon us (in 1992), we were able to celebrate by looking forward as well as through the rear-view mirror. Three exhibitions and their catalogues paid appropriate tribute to Harvard's rare book and manuscript collections, and to the librarians who brought them to Cambridge. But the year concluded with a symposium devoted to the future of special collections libraries, with speakers drawn from across the country as well as Europe. Once the proceedings had been edited and published, we sent a copy to every faculty member in the humanities and social sciences, hoping that our newly cultivated core constituency would realize that the local manor house was attempting to put its imprint on the wider world of libraries once again.

As I now look back, with some hindsight, on "my Harvard library years" (in Keyes Metcalf's familiar phrase), I am keenly aware of what we could not — or simply did not — achieve. But I can also take a certain amount of satisfaction in reminding myself of how much we actually did accomplish, and of how many of my colleagues joined forces to make Houghton a more modern and lively institution. This is not to say that we didn't encounter difficulties at many a turn. Much energy had to be devoted to rear-guard actions that would protect the library's budget and thus the size of its staff, especially during financially troubled times. I had hoped to make these efforts as invisible as possible, for I did not want my colleagues to know how hard — and how often — we were pressed; but I'm certain that many of them fully understood our situation, having experienced similar difficulties long before I joined them. I began to realize how cyclical these financial forces could be even during the brief seven and a half years of my directorship. A university as old and large and rich as Harvard could not entirely insulate its diverse constituencies from external conditions, especially the severe recession that followed the dubious "Massachusetts miracle" of the late 1980s.

Even in moments of adversity, moreover, it was important to recall the fable of the despairing father and his identical twins. Harvard (and Houghton) were not unique; other libraries were suffering or expanding or fine-tuning themselves during the 1990s. Everything we pursued was essentially in step with the aspirations of our sibling institutions. If we could occasionally demonstrate leadership in one form or another, so much the better; but if other libraries provided an attractive model (as Beinecke did with its extensive visiting-fellowship program), that was fine too. And so we completed the retrospective conversion of our book records and began to automate the records for manuscripts, prints, photographs, playbills, and other works on paper. We renovated the climate-control system, the storage areas for photographs and architectural plans, and the reading room and its environs. (Perhaps my gravestone should read, "He removed the water from the Houghton Library and put it back in the Boston Athenæum.") We raised the funding for twelve visiting fellowships and for professional development opportunities for staff members as well. Typewriters began to disappear; members of the English department began to darken our (transparent glass) doors; and *Rare Book and Manuscript Libraries in the Twenty-First Century* became, fittingly, a collectable book in its own right. The manuscript collection was still 40 percent uncataloged when I left, but that's another story, and essentially a success story at that, given the continuing dedication of my colleagues.

In the course of charting what were, for me, entirely new waters, I began to formulate a number of propositions about special collections libraries and the environments in which they operate. Grounded in my experience as an observer — as an academic *flâneur*, within my own and other institutions — these formulations were meant not so much to predict outcomes as to provoke discussion about where we were headed. I began by floating the paradoxical proposition that *the traditional library is not what it used to be*, that it can embrace prevalent forms of change without necessarily losing sight of the singularity of its identity and history.

Libraries will always be engaged in, or at least actively contemplating, changes in the way they fulfill their missions. The nature of those missions may also change, as we have seen most dramatically in the evolution of public libraries into full-service institutions within the community, offering amenities to an increasingly diverse clientele that now ranges from preschoolers to senior citizens. Traditional libraries — by which I mean institutions, like Houghton, with a strong focus on books, manuscripts, and the artistic and mechanical processes that produced them — do not pose an exception to this rule. Rare book libraries, membership libraries, and historical societies face many of the same constraints and opportunities as do their larger and more comprehensive counterparts. But when they are challenged, for example, by the advent of electronic technology, their response will be to harness it — to put it to the best possible use — and to place it in the proper perspective.

Technology should be a familiar subject to us, after all; it lies at the heart of printing and book history. The most recent revolution, dazzling as it may appear in its purported transformation of how we pursue knowledge and communicate with each other, is only the third of three. The first technological revolution, the invention of writing, continues to dwarf in importance both the development of moveable type in the mid-fifteenth century and the reconstruction of the world in bits and bytes near the close of the twentieth. A digitized image of a medieval manuscript or an early modern book may both widen and sharpen the educational process, but it cannot wholly substitute for the experience of examining the original object, or for the experience of learning from those whose job it is to pass on their hard-earned knowledge of how and why these cultural artifacts were made. Similarly, the growth of "content" on the web, extraordinary as it is, makes the *interpretation* of so much information all the more crucial. In the long run, there is still much to be said for the primal encounter between critical judgment, on the one hand, and the full spectrum of cultural production in all of its formats, on the other.

If the traditional library is no longer what it used to be (now that it has passed through the crucible of an electronic revolution), that doesn't mean that it's no longer traditional, at least in the best senses of that long-suffering word. Not unduly focused on its past, on the way things have always been done, but not forsaking its core audience and central mission as it strives to harness technology and accommodate other forms of change. I therefore felt comfortable in arguing that *almost everything we prize about our current institutions will have a place in the library of the future* — at least in the near future. The construction of websites and the digitization of texts and images are certainly not incompatible with a more traditional focus on interpretive programs — lectures, exhibitions, publications, teaching out of the collections — that have been the hallmark of so many rare book libraries during the past several decades. Many central library activities, moreover (I am thinking of acquisitions, cataloging, and reference services in particular), have already been significantly enhanced by the advent of the new technology; doubtless others will follow. Enhancement strikes me as both the most realistic and the most promising way to characterize what technology has in store for us.

The nature of the materials we collect will continue to evolve, moreover, partly because of what is available (and affordable) in the marketplace, partly because of changing patterns in scholarship. I can't imagine the great research libraries failing to strengthen their central collections whenever they can: type specimens and writing books at the Newberry Library, old-master drawings and illuminated manuscripts at the Pierpont Morgan Library, or Western Americana and early English historical papers at the Huntington. But certain new scholarly patterns have clearly emerged, particularly in the study of women, gender, sexual practices and preferences, African-American literature and history, and colonial and post-colonial history and literature. Several generations of American scholars have now heeded Mikhail Bahktin's maxim that "the most intense and productive life of culture takes place on the boundaries." The margins have now become central to the study of art, literature, and history — a development, by the way, that makes "universal" libraries as well as unpruned specialist collections look all the more prescient.

It can be difficult to know which boundaries to explore, however, and it is sometimes easy to make costly mistakes. Houghton's founding librarian, the formidable William Alexander Jackson, had no trouble in pursuing copies of early English books listed (or, better yet, unlisted) in Wing and the STC, and he was remarkably successful in convincing New Englanders to rid their attics of the seminal documents of the American Renaissance. But his decision to build a modernist collection around the Sitwell family has not sat well with later generations of curators and scholars. The challenge during my own tenure was to build upon the library's great British and American collections by developing a more international focus on contemporary writing. We were therefore cultivating New Directions and the *New Republic* with one hand while we were purchasing the manuscripts of Wole Soyinka and Chinua Achebe with the other. I was particularly interested in acquiring V. S. Naipaul's papers for Harvard, for I believed — and still do believe — that while his work is uneven, he best personifies the forces at play in contemporary culture. A writer of Indian descent raised in the Caribbean and living in England, Naipaul has trained an often scathing eye on Africa and the Americas as well as the sub-continent. We had a cordial lunch in London; I made what, for Houghton, was an unprecedented offer; but we were badly outbid by the University of Tulsa, a telling reminder of how many rivals Harvard now had.

In the long run, of course, I don't think it makes any great difference whether Naipaul's papers are in Tulsa or Cambridge; the important thing is that they are in safe keeping, properly cataloged, and accessible to the scholarly world. Competition is healthy, and no one — not even the Getty — can afford to be complacent. By collecting Achebe and Soyinka and trying to corner the market in Naipaul, we were in fact following the shrewd advice proffered by Stanley Katz during our fiftieth-anniversary symposium. Noting that rare book libraries are usually located at the center of university campuses, Katz predicted that the challenge will lie in bringing them to the center intellectually as well. Reconceptualized special collections libraries and librarians can emerge, he argued in 1992, "as significant and creative elements in the reconfigured university of the next century. Ironically, the rare books operation may move from the snob periphery to the intellectual core of the university as it behaves less as inventory than as utility, as it becomes more intellectually proactive in its behavior."

The more successfully a rare book library moves from the periphery, the more likely it is to *experience a dramatic increase — a virtual explosion — in the use of its materials.* Part of this increased demand has already been generated by unprecedented access through retrospective conversion and the growth of national bibliographic utilities, but part has almost certainly been fueled by the rise in interdisciplinary scholarship and by a renewed emphasis on research in the undergraduate curriculum. Special collections libraries can also move toward the center by taking responsibility for a wider range of historical objects. In Houghton's case, the traditional cut-off date for the automatic transfer of older books found in the stacks of Widener was 1700; by the time I left we had moved that date to 1820, roughly the end of the hand-press era, substantially enlarging our book stock and thereby increasing the conservation and preservation needs of our collections.

Progress comes at a cost. Of course it does, and not simply in financial terms, daunting as they may be. Librarians themselves will have to be part of the program. When I was involved in the extensive interviewing process before I was offered the librarianship of Houghton, I was asked a fundamental (and plangent) question by one of the curators: "What exactly are we supposed to do these days?" In years past, he explained, he had acquired materials for the library and made sure that they were properly cataloged. Now he was supposed to serve on committees, give presentations, teach courses, prepare exhibitions, and raise the money to make all of these additional activities happen. Was the acquisitions program still important? How were librarians to set priorities for themselves and their departments? How could each of these responsibilities be carried out with the care and integrity that Harvard required of its curatorial staff, that "shadow faculty" which added so much to the richness of a student's educational experience?

I had no easy answers then and few comforting answers by the time I departed. As one of my colleagues in human resources bluntly put it, "No one owns his or her own job description." Libraries are organic entities; they need to change — intelligently, carefully — if they are to survive, let alone flourish. Those who enjoy the privilege of serving in these institutions should no longer count on working within a quaint time-warp. Virtually all rare book and manuscript libraries, moreover, are at the mercy of regional as well as national economies. In Terry Belanger's shrewd formulation, each represents a national treasure that must be supported by local resources, and even the most formidable of endowments can shrink. But local resources can sometimes prove to be quite surprising, and I was occasionally pleased to learn, after failing to find external sources of funding, how many forms of support existed within the university itself. In the case of old, large, and rich Harvard, perhaps this should not actually be so surprising; often, I discovered, an institution with a certain amount of critical mass simply attracted other resources to it, as if some arcane law of cultural astrophysics were at play.

I saw this dynamic at work most vividly when the curator of manuscripts and I received an inquiry about our possible interest in a long-missing part of a letter from John Keats to his brother George and sister-in-law Georgiana in the Kentucky wilderness. Scholars had long had a text of this lengthy and important letter, which runs to 60 pages on 30 leaves, but without the entire manuscript it was impossible to determine whether that text was accurate and complete. Houghton had by far the greatest collection of Keats' holographs; the bicentenary

of his birth was just behind us, and we had mounted a beautiful exhibition and held an ambitious symposium featuring
scholars and writers from around the world. Surely the reintro-
duction of this important manuscript would represent a coup
for the library and for Harvard.

There were problems, however; serious problems. The
woman who owned the important fragment of the letter had
done so for some time. Decades earlier, when she asked where
her manuscript would find its most appropriate institutional
home, she was told by everyone she consulted that it should go
to Harvard. My great predecessor, William Jackson, arranged to
meet her in Washington, but he so thoroughly offended her
when they met that she not only decided to keep the manuscript, but also wrote scathing letters of denunciation to the
president of the university and to the two sitting senators from
the Commonwealth of Massachusetts. When I asked her on the
telephone what it was that Jackson had said to her, she replied
that Houghton's librarian insisted that her precious letter
"belonged to Harvard."

Perhaps Jackson simply said (or intended to say) that the
manuscript belonged *at* Harvard because the rest of the letter
was already there, portions of it having been given to the university by Amy Lowell and Arthur Houghton. Our potential
donor, on the other hand, had good reason to believe that the
manuscript belonged to *her*, and she was unreceptive to Jackson's manner, which she clearly thought was imperious. The
fragment had been given to her by a friend, someone who knew
that she would take good care of it after he died. She had waited
decades before exploring, for a second time, how the manuscript might best be placed in a suitable library. When she consulted a group of new advisors, she received the same advice as
before: it should really go to Cambridge. After exhausting all of

the alternatives, she finally, reluctantly, had her friends set up another conversation with haughty Houghton.

The first question she asked me over the telephone was whether William Jackson was dead. I assured her that he was, that he had in fact died three decades earlier, in 1964. She did not know this, she said, and was relieved. Would I come to see her in Arizona? I explained that my parents lived just a few miles from her, in Scottsdale, and that I was planning to visit them for the Christmas holidays; it would give me great pleasure to see her then. She asked that we meet at her local bank in Phoenix. I told her that I would be wearing a navy blazer and a moustache. She responded that she would be wearing a navy sweat suit and looked like my grandmother. We had a date.

I was the first to arrive. An officer of the bank led me to a table in a secluded part of the lobby; over the loudspeaker system I could hear Elvis quietly singing "White Christmas." When my donor arrived at the table, I realized that she had already visited her safety-deposit box, for she had the framed fragment in her hands. She was very pleased to meet me, she said, but before giving me the manuscript she wanted to ask just a few more questions. "Are you sure that William Jackson is dead," she asked? I assured her that this was the case. "Does Mr. Jackson's son work at the Houghton Library?" No, I assured her; he was a minister who taught at a theological seminary in Pittsburg. This surprised her somewhat, but not as much as her next question surprised me. "There is a certain professor at Harvard," she said, "named Walter Jackson Bate, who has written a biography of Keats. Is he related to William Jackson?" No, I assured her; Jack was a good friend, and I could vouch for his upbringing in Indiana, far from Harvard and even further from Bill Jackson's native city of San Marino.

Finally, with a smile, she placed the manuscript in my hands

— a difficult and brave gesture after more than thirty years of fretting over the unusual treasure her friend had given her. I agreed to have a beautiful photocopy made that would fit right back into the frame. I told her about the exhibition in which the rest of her manuscript had enjoyed star billing; in return she took me back to her original encounter with my detested predecessor. "Mr. Jackson looked at the letter a long time," she said, "and then he read every word aloud, so I knew something was wrong. I am sure that he was tape-recording as he read, and that he was photographing it with a secret camera when he held the letter up to the light. And then he told me that it belonged to Harvard, and I knew that I couldn't trust him." Elvis was now singing "Silent Night." I told her that it was time to let bygones be bygones; her treasure was safe with me. I walked her to her car, wished her Merry Christmas, and then quietly walked over to my own, carefully placing the framed manuscript on the seat next to me as I prepared to accompany John Keats on his rendezvous with destiny.

Chapter 2
The Scholar-Librarian

THIS ESSAY will probably irritate a number of people, especially — and ironically — those who work within American research libraries. Ironically, I suggest, because any attempt to articulate the importance of librarians pursuing independent scholarship will face pockets of resistance among those who are thought, in both the academic and the common imagination, to be the central facilitators of such research. There are those, for instance, who will argue that the battle is over. University librarians *used* to aspire towards faculty rank and status; they *used* to take pride in serving as a kind of shadow professoriate. But librarians have now set themselves apart, with their own reward systems and with technological skills that many faculty members could not begin to comprehend.

This essay, long encouraged by Terry Belanger and long deferred by the author, was written for presentation at Rare Book School at the University of Virginia in the summer of 2005. It is published here for the first time. Readers interested in related essays may wish to consult my "Predictions and Provocations," in *Rare Book and Manuscript Libraries in the Twenty-First Century*, which I edited (Cambridge MA: Harvard Univ. Library, 1993), pp. 9-13 (this collection was also issued as *Harvard Library Bulletin* NS 4.1-2 [1993]), and "Special Collections Libraries: Looking Ahead by Looking Back," *Libraries & Culture* 37 (2002): 19-25.

And then there are those who will argue that my title is redundant, that many librarians are partially or fully engaged in scholarly research by the very nature of their jobs as they catalog books (for example) or work behind a reference desk. To talk about "scholar-librarians" might be construed, by them, to be doubly insulting, for it could ignore the scholarly work they do perform while suggesting, at the same time, that what really counts is scholarly activity pursued apart from their institutional responsibilities. How much more can one ask for? And then there are those who will argue that such an argument is essentially self-serving, that it attempts to justify one's own commitment to a scholarly life by drawing attention to one's own accomplishments. Even worse, the name itself sounds old-fashioned, redolent of Arnold's scholar-gypsy, or Altick's scholar-adventurer, or (God forbid) a gentleman and a scholar. Why attempt to raise such a fusty banner in the first place?

For a number of important reasons, I shall suggest, but never for prescriptive purposes. My argument may be polemical, but it is not intended to be dogmatic. I strongly believe in the pursuit of scholarly activities by librarians, but I am not arguing that all librarians should pursue such activities. Nor do I mean to denigrate those who are not engaged in such a pursuit. Scholar-librarians are not, in my brief, elevated above their institutional colleagues; the nature of their interests is, however, sometimes misunderstood, and this essay should therefore be construed as an apology — as a classical defense — on their behalf. My remarks are addressed to those department heads, library directors, provosts, and deans who hire, promote, and reward librarians within institutional structures that are increasingly corporate and bureaucratic. Some of these libraries, as I know from my own experience, can be actively hostile towards the kind of intellectual independence such scholarly research represents. Surely it is time for clarity, if not outright détente.

Perhaps I can begin to frame my arguments by recalling a moment when I was frustratingly close to becoming a scholarly apostate. Several years ago I had an extended conversation with a good friend of mine, someone whose career trajectory has been remarkably like my own: same graduate programs, same training as a literary scholar, a similar teaching experience within a research university, and a similar experience as that university's undergraduate dean. I had become a library director, but otherwise our experiences were virtually parallel, and both of us were now lamenting the rapidly diminishing rewards that attended the publication of our scholarly work. Scholarly monographs continued to play a much more important role than journal articles within the academic community, and yet university-press books were expensive to create, slow to appear, limited in their print runs, increasingly expensive to purchase (out of the reach of most graduate students, to say nothing of our undergraduates), and reviewed so sporadically that — as Samuel Johnson complained during his years in Grub Street — they often arrived stillborn from the press. Why, under such circumstances, should we continue to knock ourselves out in order to produce books that promised so few professional rewards and generated so little academic — let alone popular — demand?

Several answers lay close to hand. At the practical end of the spectrum, because such scholarly work was expected of us, even following the trials of tenure and promotion — and promotion once again. At the more altruistic end — and as the tenure documents reminded us — because we were attempting to make an original contribution to knowledge. Or because we had been conducting research and writing critical prose for so long that it had become second nature to us: it was in our blood, and we would continue in the same manner in spite of the occasional review and the (appropriately) small print run. Each of these reasons was certainly true, but my friend contended that, in our somewhat unusual circumstances, there was an even better argument to be made: such scholarly work offered precisely what was needed "to keep us sharp."

If, as Howard Gardner has argued, there are different kinds of intelligence, surely there are also different ways to hone those intelligences in order to keep ourselves sharp. One could argue that the analytical skills involved in scholarly research, reading, and writing would not only extend our useful lives in the academy but would also ensure that we keep our wits about us well beyond middle age. But what my friend particularly had in mind was the fact that, having both entered administration, we were less actively involved than before in the analytical work of our professorial colleagues. At their best, administrative positions require a variety of interpretive (and personal) skills that might, on closer inspection, impress even the most suspicious academic. But it is also true that most scholarly work in the humanities and social sciences involves much more concentrated analysis and a much longer time-frame than do most administrative endeavors. To pursue one's scholarly life through extended research and writing therefore enables administrators (both those on temporary assignment and those who have committed themselves to life sentences) to keep their fundamental interpretive skills in good repair and — by extension — to remain in touch with the work of their academic colleagues.

I want to make precisely the same argument about those of us who work within libraries (or museums, historical societies, and other cultural institutions). Much as we might wish conditions to be otherwise, it is the rare librarian or curator indeed who pursues full-time research for his or her livelihood. Most of us who work within research libraries face a wide variety of tasks even if our position bears a seemingly single-minded title such as "rare book cataloger" or "paper conservator." Every cataloger or conservator I have known has been asked (or required) to participate in a sometimes frustrating hodgepodge of activities: training sessions, search committees, advisory boards, review panels, lecture and publication committees, task forces, strategic planning, even (God forbid) institutional downsizing. Every reader of this essay can easily augment my profoundly un-Homeric list. At the Boston Athenæum we actually add the phrase "other duties as may be required" to the description of each of our positions — and we mean it, especially when cooperation between or among departments is needed.

Because of the variety of activities most of us are asked to undertake, it is therefore all the more important that the central responsibilities of each position be clearly defined and successful performance be properly rewarded. Rare-book catalogers who are frequently asked to serve on search committees and technology task forces are — at some point — likely to be personally frustrated and professionally unfulfilled as well as relatively unproductive. Those of us who take managerial responsibility for such positions and performances must either revise our criteria for a job well done or (better yet, I think) protect those central activities from being eroded by all of the other duties our colleagues are asked to carry out. Curators, for example, are trained (and train themselves) to perform a number of critical tasks; it is essential that they be provided with the time, resources, and moral support to be as successful — and creative — as possible.

I doubt whether many librarians will quarrel with the proposition I have just made, although some may find it relatively Panglossian during a dry economic season such as the one we are still currently enduring. It is clearly another thing, however, to argue that colleagues who are already encumbered by the burdens and diversions I have described should also pursue their own research at the same time. How might we make that happen? I propose two interrelated components in a program that should provide the working conditions for independent scholarship in a library setting.

First, those who pursue (or aspire to pursue) their own scholarship must sense that they do so within a safe environment. Library directors and their senior managers must follow a common course, articulating the same goals and sending consistent signals to those around them. Nothing is more insidious than the sense (real or perceived) that "senior management" considers such scholarship to be unnecessary or, worse yet, inappropriate. I know first-hand what that environment feels like, having experienced it together with my colleagues during a particular rocky moment at Harvard. A number of librarians wished to form a discussion group in which they could talk about their "outside" scholarly interests on a regular (and somewhat formal) basis. The institutional well was so quickly and effectively poisoned, however, that it took years for this enterprise to take root — and when it did, it took the form of a consortium of librarians from a variety of local libraries. The Ticknor Society, as it is known, has proven to be quite successful, but its birth-pangs (at least among Harvard's librarians) were not easy.

An appropriate environment for such a society (and the scholarship that underlies it) needs more than reassuring lip-service, however: it must also reside on the bedrock of institutional support and rewards, the second component in what I consider to be a modest and manageable proposal. By support I specifically mean funding for professional development. Financial resources devoted to professional development represent one of the most cost-effective measures a cultural institution can take. The price-tag can be surprisingly low, and a small investment can produce disproportionately large results. Release time for independent work, for instance, costs nothing in financial terms and, rather than vitiating an institution's "productivity," can actually work to increase it, as I shall argue later. Simple flexibility in determining a colleague's schedule can often obviate the question of paid release time; but even when that is not the case, the occasional leave — whether it be a week, a month, or an extended sabbatical — will easily make up in one way (staff morale, loyalty to the institution, intellectual rejuvenation, contributions to scholarly knowledge) what it may appear to lose in other terms. I would wager, moreover, that many staff members would be happy to put up with the disruption caused by a colleague's temporary absence if they knew that similar opportunities were available to them as well.

Even when actual dollars are on the table, the relative cost can be astonishingly modest. During my tenure at the Houghton Library, a windfall of $10,000 was offered to me if I could mount an effective argument for its use. The proposal I made was not immediately greeted with enthusiasm, but in the long run I eventually prevailed: each year, for five years, two members of the Houghton staff would receive a full-paid, one-month leave and a stipend of $1,000 to work on a scholarly project of their choice. Senior members of the staff joined me in choosing the two winners during the first year's competition, and those who received awards joined me on the selection committee thereafter.

The program eventually encompassed one-third of the library's staff, but even those who did not apply for one of these fellowships realized that the pursuit of scholarly projects was consonant with the mission of the library as a whole.

The dedication of $2,000 to this program within an annual library budget of over $3 million was a mere drop in the bucket (or, as they say at Harvard, a droplet in a tublet on its own bottomlet). The program was so effective that I immediately sought to replicate it when I arrived at the Boston Athenæum, and — thanks to enlightened funding from a family closely allied with the library and strongly committed to the support of scholarly research — we were soon able to launch a series of ten Wellspring Fellowships for a staff of roughly fifty members. This time round, moreover, I broadened the terms of the competition to encompass original creative work (fiction, sculpture, and the book arts, for example) as well as time spent as a visiting fellow at another cultural institution. The original ten fellowships have all been awarded, and we now fund the program on a permanent basis. Surely an annual commitment of $1,000 within a budget of almost $6 million should not be hard to sustain, let alone to justify. Scholarly support of this kind, modest as it is, will stretch even further so long as it is used for tax-exempt purposes. More ambitiously, an institution can offer continuing research accounts for staff members as well as book subventions that will assist colleagues in negotiating with a scholarly press.

But why, to return to my initial point of departure, should investments such as these be made? In addition to the rather intangible rewards I have mentioned — staff morale, staying sharp, contributions to scholarly knowledge — there are tangible benefits as well. Perhaps the most important lies in the fact that scholar-librarians normally pursue their research in a number of repositories and therefore learn, through that scholarly process, how other institutions work. This process begins long before an actual visit is made. In order to define their projects (and apply for support) scholar-librarians need to determine where relevant research materials can be found and how easily they can be accessed, steps that essentially place them in the role of visitors to their *own* institution. They will soon learn how effective other websites are, how other electronic catalogs are structured, whether visiting fellowships are available, whether access to certain materials is restricted, what forms of introduction and identity are required, whether laptops and personal materials are allowed in the reading rooms, whether there is an orientation to the library and its collections, and what kinds of resources are offered to visiting scholars (lockers, photocopying, lounges, access to curators, the services of a reference staff — all of the amenities, both large and small, that help determine the success of each individual scholar's visit).

There is no effective substitute for a visit of this kind, not even an extensive tour provided by an obliging colleague. You have to participate in an orientation meeting and then work within the library itself in order to gauge how effective your introduction has been — let alone how comparatively effective such sessions are at your home institution. It takes time to determine how well another library's catalog and delivery system work, or how knowledgeable and helpful staff members are. Institutions cannot be fully evaluated from the outside. In the process of pursuing their own research, scholar-librarians are simultaneously learning about their host and their home institutions, and it has been my experience that they return with a clearer sense of their own library's strengths and weaknesses. Their suggestions will not always be accepted, but they will — at the very least — have provoked the right kinds of discussion.

Colleagues who pursue their own scholarship also bring another tangible asset to their home institutions, which is first-hand knowledge of how scholarship in their particular fields is being pursued. Methodologies (and even ideologies) are constantly being revised and reformulated, and it does no one any good to turn his or her back on such developments. Librarians may sometimes view the fashions of the current academic catwalk with healthy skepticism, but such skepticism must be grounded in a clear understanding of contemporary issues and the cultural stakes attached to them. Librarians working at colleges and universities have an obligation, in my view, to know *how* their professorial colleagues are thinking in order to be able to support their scholarship and teaching. And if it is important for academic librarians to stay intellectually tuned in, it might conversely be argued that this obligation is even greater for librarians at non-academic institutions that also support research. Without teachers and students constantly putting a library's resources to use, it is more difficult — and therefore more important — for at least some librarians to remain part of the larger scholarly conversation.

It has been my experience that independent research and the scholarly interludes that support it actually refresh (rather than overburden) individual librarians, providing them with a break in their professional routines and, in many cases, a salutary perspective on how to juggle their various duties and obligations. It is also important to remember that when one's colleagues pursue their research in other libraries, attend conferences, and share their scholarship orally and in print, they are simultaneously representing their home institutions. Among other things, they are implicitly (and sometimes explicitly) informing the scholarly world that scholarship is valued at their libraries — and this is knowledge that is not lost on other librarians as they consider which positions to apply for. Vigorous (and visible) institutional support for professional development therefore represents an attractive resource as a library seeks to make the strongest possible appointments to its staff.

And now another seeming paradox, which is that independent research and publication not only allow individuals to represent their institutions, but enable them to represent *themselves* as well. This may sound like heresy to some library directors, but I think that it is important for our professional colleagues to be able to speak for themselves as well as for us. Much library work, after all, is collaborative by nature. We rightly value intelligent teamwork, often to the point where individual effort is not even explicitly acknowledged. (How many times have I had to insist that a curator or editor's name be printed on the title-page and spine of a book!) It is psychologically healthy for librarians, or at least for some librarians, to know that they have a life apart from their institutional role, that they alone could shape a particular scholarly argument or discover a particular scholarly treasure, that their name alone could grace a particular essay or monograph. And what is true for our colleagues is perhaps even more important for library directors themselves, who are even more closely associated with their institutions. I'm personally pleased and amused when one of our members salutes me in Boston as "Mr. Athenæum," but it is psychologically helpful for me to possess an identity separate from — and, as I have argued, also contributing to — my life at 10½ Beacon Street.

I began this essay by suggesting that, among the many other things it does, the continuing pursuit of your scholarly interests has the fundamental virtue of keeping you sharp. It also keeps you young, in the sense that research, reading, and writing draw one into an intellectual conversation that is constantly renewed by the influx of younger scholars. But there is also much to be said for the knowledge (and occasional wisdom) that come with years of extended reading and research. My respect for my senior colleagues at the Houghton Library — and my conviction that they should continue to be able to contribute to the life of our enterprise — led me into more than a little hot water during my Harvard library years. I thought that it would make good sense to offer certain retiring members of the staff (curators and catalogers with extensive knowledge of our collections) an opportunity to continue their work on individual library projects: cataloging single-page European manuscripts, for example, or illustrated eighteenth-century Italian books. There was already a precedent for such a maneuver; I was simply institutionalizing it on a more extensive basis.

Needless to say, my colleagues in the Harvard College Library were not amused. I was reminded that retirement was, by its very nature, supposed to clear the way for new blood, that allowing senior members of the staff to remain at Houghton would impede the work of their successors. These were intelligent reservations, but I believed that such an arrangement would work if the ground rules were clear enough. And so I created what I called Houghton Heaven — and what the outside world, I later learned, called Valhalla. Certain librarians didn't actually retire; they simply moved to even grander quarters upstairs. I displayed my faith in them, and they demonstrated their respect for me by following my one commandment, which was that those who worked in Houghton Heaven must behave angelically. Don't interfere with the work of your successor; don't confuse your colleagues about who's actually in charge; and, most importantly, don't tell me how to do my job. I cannot say, in retrospect, that this arrangement was perfect. I can say, however, that in a society that increasingly treats both traditional forms of knowledge and older generations with scant respect, we did our best to buck the tide. Virtually every space within the library was alive with library business and — as you will have guessed — with individual projects as well.

When the English painter Thomas Gainsborough was dying, he turned to his arch-rival, Sir Joshua Reynolds, and said, "We're all going to heaven, and Van Dyck will be of the company." This is a comforting thought, I suppose, but I would rather strive to create heaven here on earth, or at least within the confines of the institutions in which I've had the privilege to work. I am aware, of course, that what is one person's heaven can also constitute another person's hell, but the doctrine I have attempted to preach in this essay is one of mutual respect and understanding. Librarians deserve all the respect and support we can give them, and no matter which metaphors we may choose to characterize their contributions to our culture — as bearers of the keys to knowledge, as loyal keepers of the flame — the roles they perform are central to our understanding of the societies in which we live. I am not arguing that those keys, those flames, lie solely in the hands of scholar-librarians; but I am suggesting, as strongly as I can, that scholar-librarians perform essential roles within each institution in which we are fortunate enough to find and nurture them.

Chapter 3
Living with Piranesi

I N THE SPRING OF 1984, as I was slowly resolving to become a better educated and more disciplined print collector, I screwed up my courage and pushed against the thick plate-glass door that led to Stanley Johnson's gallery on Chicago's Michigan Avenue. I had meant to do so for some time, but the gallery looked so elegant, so sophisticated — so grown-up, I suppose — that I had only glimpsed its interior as I was heading in or out of another suite on the second floor of the same building. Stanley himself, as it turned out, was just as forbidding as his gallery: crisp, intense, immaculately tailored,

---

My wife Elizabeth and I mounted an exhibition of prints in our collection at the request of the South Shore Art Center in Cohasset, Massachusetts, in January 2004. When I mentioned our show, entitled "Piranesi and His Contemporaries," to Carol Rothkopf at a Grolier Club luncheon, she asked me to consider writing an essay about my experiences as a collector. This chapter first appeared in the *Gazette of the Grolier Club* 55 (2004) and is closely tied to Chapter 5 in this volume, "Piranesi's Double Ruin." Collecting has, of course, become an important critical subject with an extensive literature devoted to it. See, for instance, *The Cultures of Collecting*, edited by John Elsner and Roger Cardinal (Cambridge MA: Harvard Univ. Press, 1994), which includes Jean Baudrillard's seminal essay "The System of Collecting," and Susan M. Pearce, *On Collecting* (London and New York: Routledge, 1995).

flanked by assistants and a beautiful German wife. The gallery was spare and deserted, and there was no place to hide. Although Stanley's greeting was cordial enough, he was obviously curious about a young stranger who was not nearly as crisp, intense, or immaculately tailored as he was. What was my name? What was I interested in? What could he show me?

On his walls was an exhibition devoted to European printmaking ranging from the work of Dürer and Cranach to that of Bresdin and Picasso. I have never, in the past twenty years, seen a more impressive show outside the walls of a museum, unless (of course) it was in Stanley's own gallery. I attempted to explain that I was very much an amateurish collector, that I had a few prints by Hogarth, but that I was trying to educate my eye (without immediately flattening my slender wallet). "Hogarth," he exclaimed; yes, there was an engraving by Hogarth in the exhibition, just one (the charming *Strolling Actresses Dressing in a Barn*). Hogarth wasn't a great printmaker, he explained, but he was fun. "Make yourself at home." I pretended to, of course, but as soon as I could take a polite powder I quickly fled.

But I also returned, for the prints on the walls were astonishingly beautiful. Executed by different artists working in different countries at different times and in different media, they nevertheless shared the common representational challenge of working with the brashness or subtlety of black and grey ink on a light and unforgiving ground. Stanley walked me around the gallery and spoke with precision and passion about what made individual images so special: a Goya, a Rosa, a Tiepolo. When we had completed our circuit, he turned to me and delivered the following parable: "If you invited me to visit your apartment, and when I arrived I discovered that you had nothing hanging in your foyer, or in your living room, or in your library — nothing hanging in the dining room, nothing in the corridor — but that you had a small etching by Rembrandt hanging in your bedroom, I would shake you by the hand and say, 'Congratulations! *You* have a first-rate art collection.'"

Advice it was, advice from which both explicit and implicit lessons might be drawn. The generous, explicit moral was that you didn't have to possess many works of art in order to have a collection of integrity and value. The reverse side of Stanley's coin suggested a rather different lesson, however, for it was clear that he preferred empty rooms and bare walls to second-rate works of art. Would he have valued a collection comprising one etching by Rembrandt and several dozen engravings by Hogarth? I doubt it; and my predicament, of course, was that I possessed the Hogarths but not the Rembrandt. To make matters worse, Stanley then asked me what I did for a living. I answered, with what I hoped was hidden satisfaction, that I was a professor of English literature at Northwestern — an eighteenth-century scholar, in fact. Stanley looked as disappointed as anyone I've ever met. "Academics are the worst possible collectors," he replied. "Instead of buying what is beautiful, you invariably buy what you think is interesting."

As I look back on these encounters twenty years later, I must confess that I have fallen painfully short of Stanley's standards for collecting. My house is neat and tidy, but it is also filled with a large number of *things*, very few of which rival the value or beauty of that single Dutch etching hanging in a bedroom in which I shall never sleep. I'm not an undisciplined person; far from it, I'm afraid. But I shall never rival a fastidious colleague of mine who had no furniture at all in his living room because he couldn't afford any of the pieces he approved of.

It is true that I have disposed of all but one of my Hogarths, but the narrow, Spartan path that leads to a single Rembrandt is not for me. I collect what I find to be both interesting *and* attractive, and I take special pleasure in purchasing (and often rehabilitating) what others may have overlooked: a cropped Audubon less valuable than its uncut siblings but more attractive precisely because of its more compact "window"; a smoke-black mezzotint of the painter Benjamin West, rescued from a crumbling frame, crisply matted in white, protected by antique glass and a gold-leaf frame rubbed slightly red; a black-ink drawing almost three feet wide and two feet high that enigmatically fuses a plan and elevation into "A Water Source" (1933), which I am almost certain was modeled by an aspiring English architect after various experiments by Piranesi in the *Antichità Romane.*

How can I be so sure? Because I've lived with Piranesi for the past twenty years. He's to be found virtually everywhere in our house, including the bedroom in which I *do* sleep at night. His portrait stares across our living room at the cropped Audubon; his architectural plans-and-elevations are set against the deep red walls of our small sitting room, and his son Francesco's *Borghese Gladiator* guards the master bath. I think that Stanley Johnson might possibly approve, for much of that handsome exhibition in Chicago in 1984 was devoted to Piranesi — almost an entire room, as I now reconstruct it from memory. Never before had I seen such variety from the hand of a single artist. Many of the prints were delicate evocations of a silvery Roman world rendered with a light, almost feathery touch. In stark contrast, other etchings explored the dark nether-world of the *Carceri*, rendered through intense inking and dramatic chiaroscuro. These are the prints that led Marguerite Yourcenar to explore the "dark brain" of Piranesi; these are the images in which my friend Joseph Roach has noted the "chilling paradox" of prisons "to which there are no precise boundaries, yet from which there is no escape."

I was enthralled. There *was* no escape. Piranesi was tantalizingly familiar — in the sense that he was an eighteenth-century artist — but he was simultaneously exotic and remote. He was Italian in the first place, of course, and I knew absolutely nothing about Venice and Rome in the *Settecento*. I had begun my scholarly career, moreover, by focusing on the ways in which mid-eighteenth-century poetry, particularly the work of William Collins and Thomas Gray, served as a linguistic and cultural bridge between the high Augustan irony of Alexander Pope and the full-blown romanticism of Wordsworth and Coleridge. *My* eighteenth century faced forwards. Piranesi's eighteenth century, on the other hand, was manifestly neoclassical; it looked backwards even when he was envisioning new buildings that might be erected in the Eternal City. Here, then, was a fresh world to explore, a world (as I would eventually discover) that encompassed classical scholarship, architectural history, theatrical scene design, the Grand Tour, and the intricacies of the etching process itself.

But how to begin? I'm certain that Stanley Johnson realized that I couldn't afford the prints in his gallery even before I did. I mentioned my nascent interest to Russell Maylone, the curator of special collections at Northwestern. Had I ever heard of the dealer Lettario Calapai, he asked? Lettario Calapai! The name was too good to be true, and I therefore quickly followed up with a telephone call and a trip north to Glencoe, where Leo (as he was called — and you can imagine why) welcomed me on a chilly Saturday morning. Russell had informed me that Leo was a very distinguished printmaker, much admired by collectors of contemporary art. What Russell didn't tell me (perhaps because he had never put himself in my supplicating position) was that Leo was essentially a print collector rather than a print dealer. He wanted his visitors to appreciate the sheets in his collection; only occasionally, when the spirit (or his bank account)

FIGURE 1.
Giovanni Battista Piranesi, *Veduta dell'Anfiteatro Flavio ditto il Colosseo,* etching, from the *Antichità Romane* (1756). Private collection.

moved him, would he actually sell (perhaps I should say deaccession) one of his prints.

My Saturday morning adventures therefore unfolded in the following manner. The first hour or so would be devoted to admiring Leo's current work, which usually involved a multiple-printing process on a large press in the middle of his studio. Sometimes he would actually be engaged in printing and I would help him move his oversized sheets on and off the press. Then he would share his treasures with me, never mentioning whether any of them might be for sale. Finally, donning my coat and pretending to leave, I would quietly ask if he might be willing to sell a particular image. The answer was usually no, but he did part with the eight plates of Hogarth's *Rake's Progress,* which I then put to good use in my courses, and Gillray's satirical print of *Titianus Redivivus,* in which the deceased Sir Joshua Reynolds comes back to life in order to discover Titian's secret coloring techniques.

Living with Piranesi proved to be more difficult. Leo certainly owned a good number of them, but they were his particular favorites, and he consulted all the auction catalogues in
order to calculate the current value of each etching. Eventually, and with some reluctance, he decided that he would part
with one image, a small etching of the Colosseum from the
Antichità Romane (figure 1). It was one of the happiest
moments in my life. Later, when I myself deaccessioned the
Hogarths and the Gillray, I discovered that, despite Leo's
protestations, they were not lifetime impressions. No matter. I
had enjoyed them for a long time, had shared them with several generations of students, and could now afford to invest
once again in Piranesi. And the *Colosseum*, as it turned out,
was "all right" (as my colleague Roger Stoddard likes to phrase
it). I bought a decent frame and proudly displayed the etching
as the only object sitting on my mantelpiece. It wasn't a Rembrandt but it *was* a beginning.

Now that I was properly launched, I gradually introduced
myself to various print dealers both here and in England. There
were quite a few at the time, even in Chicago, and I soon became
friends with David Gee, who worked out of a wonderfully ram-
shackle apartment and studio perched at the top of a building
on North Wells Street. Like Leo Calapai, David turned out to be
a collector who would occasionally sell prints he actually valued
himself: not the Piranesi in the bedroom, of course, nor the portrait of Giambattista that hung in his studio, but eventually a
lovely, small etching by Legros that I bought precisely because it
was beautiful rather than interesting.

Much more to my nascent taste for the neoclassical was an
intriguing title-page to one of the four volumes devoted to Sir
William Hamilton's collection of antique vases. Handsomely
printed in black and then hand-colored using terracotta-tinted

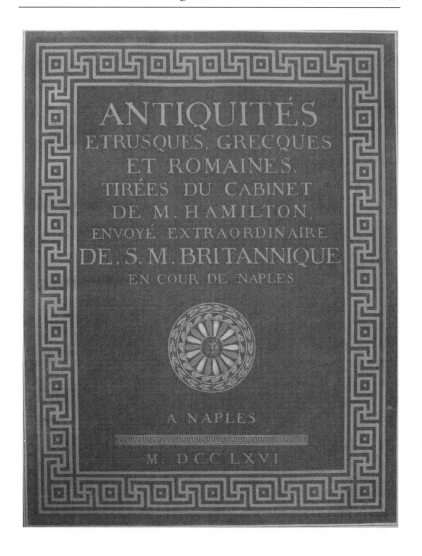

FIGURE 2.
Title-page, *Collection of Etruscan, Greek, and Roman Antiquities from the Cabinet of the Hon.ble Wm. Hamilton, His Britannick Majesty's Envoy Extraordinary at the Court of Naples,* hand-colored engraving, vol. 1 (1766 [1767]). Private collection.

ink, the title-page was one of eight plates, four in French and four in English, that introduced readers to the sumptuous volumes produced for Hamilton by the self-styled Baron d'Hancarville. I had already seen several of the engravings of the Greek and Etruscan vases themselves, but not the striking title-pages with their dramatic Greek-key motifs within the elaborate borders (figure 2). David loved the print just as much as I did; would he part with it? Eventually, yes; who else, after all, could possibly share his interest in such an unusual image? And it didn't hurt that I was a fellow Iowan, willing to listen to David talk about his early years in rural America. David was also a conservator, mat-cutter, and framer, and thus my eight Hogarths were entrusted to him along with the Hamiltonian singleton. (Many years later I discovered all *eight* of the title-pages, in pristine condition, in a small gallery in London; they had been consigned to the attic because, as the incredulous dealer told me, "we didn't think anyone would be interested in them.")

If you have followed my tale this far, you can surely discern a pattern beginning to emerge. Because I didn't have the capital to walk into a gallery like Stanley Johnson's and choose from among a variety of beautiful impressions, I had — of necessity — begun to develop alternative sources in the marketplace of art. Leo and David did not think of themselves as dealers; one was an artist, the other was a paper conservator, and both were collectors. But a good deal of patience and an interest in their own work occasionally secured me engravings that I couldn't otherwise have afforded. In addition, of course, I had everything to learn — about the market as well as the prints themselves — and my conversations with both men gave me genuine pleasure, for we shared a passion that appealed to few other fellow-travelers. This is not to say that I was bottom-fishing, as they say in the real-estate market. My goal was not to buy low and sell high, but rather to establish a corpus of good impressions of Piranesi's work by purchasing the best images available at a reasonable price. Some dealers, moreover, turned out to be affordable, particularly in London, which boasted a number of shops devoted to old-master prints twenty years ago: Craddock and Barnard, Schuster, Sotheran (in two locations), Christopher Mendez, and Robert Douwma and Ben Weinreb (sometimes together, sometimes apart).

Like many collectors in the early stages of their careers, I began by trying to find representative images of an artist's major works. In Piranesi's case, this meant the large etchings of Roman views, the *vedute* he continued to produce throughout his lifetime. I found one (a really splendid impression) at an antiques show in Chicago; I later purchased a second from Christopher Mendez and eventually a third from Sotheran. Then, in 1986, when I was attending the exhibition and symposium devoted to Sir Joshua Reynolds at the Royal Academy in London, I discovered that Ben Weinreb was offering what seemed like *all* of Piranesi in a new gallery located behind the British Museum: 193 prints as well as the entire *Antichità Romane* in four volumes. This turned out to be an unnerving (and, eventually, a backbone-stiffening) event, for it was possible to choose from virtually all of the major series: the *Prima Parte*, the *Vedute di Roma*, the *Opere Varie*, the four *Grotteschi*, and the late, dark etchings devoted to the ruins at Paestum.

With virtually all of Piranesi's world lying open before me, how was I to choose? I made two important decisions that afternoon. First, realizing that I could *just* afford a copy of one of the more important *vedute* from the early nineteenth-century Paris edition but *not* one from the contemporary editions printed in Rome, I decided to wait, to defer — perhaps the most painful decision a collector ever makes, for collectors are rarely connoisseurs of delayed gratification. I realized, however, that the advice I had received from Stanley should be brought into play at this point. Lifetime impressions of Piranesi's work are appreciably superior to the copies his son Francesco printed after he moved to Paris and became François; this was one of the visible lessons such a comprehensive exhibition could easily instill. And so I decided to collect only etchings printed before Piranesi's death in 1778. It was not, after all, a case of not being able to display any furniture in my living room, for there were many other prints, from many other series, from which to choose.

My other decision that cold February afternoon might not so easily have pleased Stanley Johnson. Realizing, as I surveyed the scores of prints on the walls, that *everything* seemed beautiful to me, I decided to purchase what I found most interesting. I already had a small Colosseum, so to speak, and three handsome *vedute*; why not begin to be as experimental in my collecting as Piranesi himself was in his printmaking? And thus began the second phase in my life as a collector as I turned my attention to frontispieces, title-pages, and initial letters, an interest already whetted by my painstakingly slow acquisition of the odd "Hamilton" and conveniently aided and abetted by my own work as a literary scholar. In addition to several conventional etchings from the *Antichità Romane*, I therefore left the gallery with an impression of Piranesi's title-page to the *Prima Parte* of 1743, his first collection of prints to be issued in codex form (figure 3).

The odd title-page, frontispiece, and *letterina* followed, and then — about eight years ago — I took a third step as a *collecteur piranesien* by purchasing a number of large architectural subjects that combine plan, elevation, and various legends and inscriptions in an unusual format. It might be said that title-

FIGURE 3.
Giovanni Battista Piranesi, title-page, *Prima Parte di Architetture, e Prospettive*, etching (fourth state, 1748 and after). Private collection.

pages and studies of capital roman letters break the traditional (and naïve) illusion of artistic realism by introducing elements from two complementary (or competing) semiotic systems: one linguistic, the other more purely visual. The linguistic element is usually subordinate, embedded within the larger visual field but also contributing to it. In the title-page to the *Prima Parte*, for instance, the figures near the center of the etching are pointing to letters that have almost entirely disappeared. In Piranesi's studies of initial letters, the capital "N" or "L" or "S" is the center of the viewer's focus, but the letter is rendered as an architectural element, part of a larger ensemble within the visual field.

In the etchings that combine plans and elevations as well as inscriptions and legends, Piranesi takes this assault on "realistic" printmaking one step further. It is impossible — or at least exceedingly difficult — to read an inscription while simultaneously perceiving the entire image within which it is embedded. It is correspondingly impossible — or at least exceedingly difficult — to study a plan and an elevation at the same time. When these two forms of competing discourse are then combined in the same image, Piranesi's viewers are required to undertake an even more complicated process of interpretation. The image can no longer be "taken in" at one time, or from one perspective, as was the case with the diminutive Colosseum. Different semiotic elements demand different "ways of looking" that must then be integrated in order to make sense of the complexity (and playfulness) of Piranesi's designs.

Forced to turn out the beautiful but conventional *vedute* throughout his lifetime in order to make a proper living as an artist, Piranesi might be thought to have turned to these other, highly unusual compilations as a welcome form of experimentation and release. Unless, of course, we look even more closely

FIGURE 4.
Giovanni Battista Piranesi, *Veduta dell'avanzo del Portico di M. Emilio Lepido*, etching, from the *Antichità Romane* (1756). Private collection.

at those etchings that I've characterized as conventional, for Piranesi is full of surprises. His first collected etchings, in the *Prima Parte*, may appear at first glance to be straightforward renderings of classical ruins and neoclassical buildings, but they are in fact designs for structures that have not yet been built (even though some of them have already decayed). Each *veduta* contains a cartouche, usually found at the bottom edge of the plate block, which contains information about the buildings depicted above. These are semantic enclaves, visually separated from the mimetic image; but they often take the form of an architectural fragment, and they always contain letters (A, B, C, D) that can also be found in the image proper. (It would be difficult, in fact, to find an etching by Piranesi that did not contain

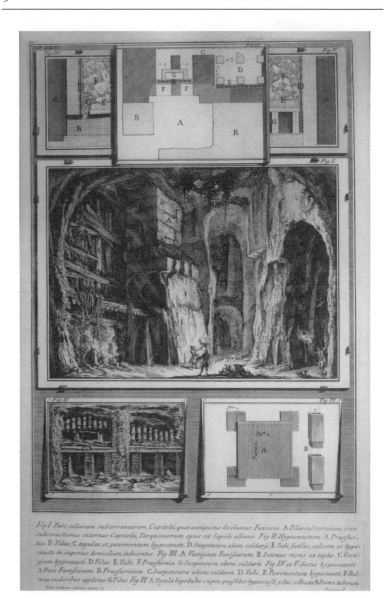

lettering of one kind or another, and some of his title-pages and dedications contain virtually nothing *but* carved inscriptions.) In some examples, as in the *Veduta dell'avanzo del Portico di M. Emilio Lepido*, from the *Antichità Romane*, the cartouche actually breaks through the lower edge of the picture, puncturing the otherwise realistic illusion of the etching and even casting a shadow on the lettering below (figure 4).

The kinds of images that I have acquired in this third phase of collecting can therefore be thought of as Piranesi's even more radical attempts to explore the visual syntax of the plate block. That he took self-conscious delight in exploding conventions and poking fun at traditional illusionism can be gauged, at least in part, by his penchant for presenting so many of these elements as prints-within-prints, as curling documents pinned to other documents. Some of these images, as in the *Pars cellarum subterranearum Capitolii* from the *Campo Marzio*, which I discovered at a local antiques show outside of Boston (figure 5), suggest that the etching is not so much devoted to certain buildings as it is to the props and paraphernalia of architectural practice. Doomed to be an architect *manqué*, with only a few projects to his credit, Piranesi could nonetheless re-create the texture of an architect's life both in the subject of his etchings and in their self-referentiality.

The frustration of living in Rome at a moment when great architectural commissions could not be had must have been particularly galling to someone with Piranesi's talent and pride. It is therefore not surprising that, by all accounts, he was not a person with whom it was easy to live. A jealous husband, a demanding father, an irascible polemicist, he was quite adept at biting the hand of the patron who fed him. We are much more fortunate today, now that the passion and the overarching ambition have been distilled into the silvery tones produced by paper, ink, and copperplate. Aristocrats, he once noted, are the latest in their lineage whereas artists are the first in theirs. Piranesi clearly understood his place in the history of printmaking as he forsook his draftsman's pencil for the etching needle.

One of the virtues, and pleasures, of living with Piranesi today is that the images themselves speak so eloquently on his behalf. In saying this, I am not referring to the inscriptional elements in his prints so much as his ability to engage his viewers in the process of interpretation. I have felt this most strongly as I have pondered the forces at work in the intriguing title-page to the *Prima Parte* (figure 3). For a long time I took simple enjoyment in speculating about these shadowy figures as they gesticulated on my living-room wall. What were they pointing to? Why was the large marble tablet near the center of the composition partially obscured by a low, rolling mist?

Following the publication of Andrew Robison's magisterial catalogue of the early imaginative "fantasies," however, I suddenly realized that the print I owned was in fact the fourth state of the first edition — and that the first and second states presented dramatically different images. Why, I then asked myself, did Piranesi only introduce human figures in later states of the etching? And why did these figures emerge only when the engraved inscription on the marble tablet began to disappear? I articulated my answers to these questions in an exploratory essay entitled "Piranesi's Double Ruin," and in doing so I began to speculate as well about the particular affinity between the subject of so much of Piranesi's work (his predilection for representing buildings in ruinous states) and the corrosive nature of the etching process itself. If I have made any contribution at all to the critical understanding of Piranesi's achievement as an artist, it lies, I believe, in my insistence on linking the physical

FIGURE 6.
Giovanni Battista Piranesi, *Tempio antico*, etching, from the *Prima Parte*
(first state, 1748). Private collection.

process and aesthetic effects of etching with Piranesi's lifelong interest in the decay and dissemination of classical culture.

Once I had published "Piranesi's Double Ruin," I sent copies of the essay to several of the print dealers who had befriended me in recent years. One of them, Michael Finney — whose eponymous gallery is to be found on Museum Street in London, near the late quarters of both The Print Room and Craddock and Barnard — asked if I would like to examine a print he had recently purchased: "it's a dirty thing, but *you* might find it interesting," as he playfully put it (figure 6). And indeed I did, even though I couldn't immediately determine what it actually was. Once I had recourse to Robison's catalogue and to some helpful magnification, however, I realized that the "dirty" sheet was a scratch-proof impression of one of the plates added to the *Prima Parte* late in the 1740s. What I had in my hands, in other words, was one of Piranesi's rare working copies of a print-in-progress — his "foul paper," so to speak, complete with the prick holes indicating that he had pinned it to a board or easel as he calibrated the lettering at the bottom of the print. The second state of this etching devoted to the elaborate, imaginary interior of an ancient temple would in time become one of Piranesi's most influential designs, and I was delighted a few months later when I discovered a beautiful impression of it in Russ Gerard's gallery on Charles Street, just a few blocks from the Boston Athenæum. All I now lack, of course, is a copy of the first state before the lettering, a print whose pursuit should keep me occupied for many years.

The proof-sheet that now hangs next to the second state of the *Tempio antico* in our bedroom is a dirty thing indeed; it would certainly be out of place in a Madison (or Michigan) Avenue gallery, and that's fine with me. My wife Elizabeth, who is a paper conservator, agreed with me that it should not be cleaned: foul papers, like sleeping dogs, shouldn't be disturbed. It's comforting, after all, to know that these odd remnants from the printing house have actually survived after two and a half centuries. Walter Benjamin's sense of the "aura" surrounding original or unique artifacts is rather too grand a conception to impose on such a slight survivor, but the scratch-proof impression nevertheless brings us a step closer to the material world in which Piranesi worked as an etcher.

So, of course, do the surviving drawings from Piranesi's hand, most of them now housed in great institutional collections. I have only acquired one additional drawing myself, a fine but anonymous rendering of the bust of a classical figure, probably a statue in the collection of the Royal Academy at the close of the eighteenth century; it hangs immediately above Piranesi's own portrait in our living room. Piranesi's own drawings rarely appear in the auction houses, and when they do they naturally fetch prices well beyond the reach of ordinary collectors such as I. With the exception of the detailed designs executed near the end of his life at Paestum, Piranesi's drawings tend to be rather unfinished. "I realize that the complete drawing isn't on my drawing paper," he confessed to his fellow *ruiniste* Hubert Robert; "however, it is very much in my head and you will see it in its entirety on my etching plate." His advice was to "go slowly," for in producing one etching "I am really in the midst of executing three thousand drawings all at the same time."

Johann Winckelmann, who argued at such length with Piranesi over the origins of Roman culture, believed that "just as the first pressing of the grapes gives the most exquisite wine, so the . . . sketch on paper of the draughtsman affords us the true spirit of the artist." I also admire and enjoy the work of great draftsmen, but I do so on aesthetic rather than vaguely metaphysical grounds. My own mentor, Charles Ryskamp, has assembled a remarkable collection of drawings, a collection rich in quality as well as range. But any collection of drawings — or of paintings, for that matter — strikes me as somewhat promiscuous in comparison with the clarity and chasteness I value in old-master prints.

My wife Elizabeth takes a very different view of this matter, to say the least. Why, she often asks, can't we introduce a little more color onto the walls that surround us? My answer, of course, is that we should paint the walls, not the art. But living with me, after all, is probably even more difficult than living with Giambattista, and living with both of us is certainly not for the faint of heart. Whatever collecting is — avocation, aspiration, sublimation, illness, grounds for divorce or disinheritance — it is also one of the most significant ways in which we express the values by which we live. I, for one, continue to count myself fortunate that I had the temerity, two decades ago, to push past the plate-glass door and sample the treasures within.

∂, Part Two ∂,

Chapter 4
Manuscripts, Mazes, and Pope's Essay on Man

In examining familiar things we come to such
unfamiliar conclusions that our very language
is twisted and bent even as it guides us.
Writing "under erasure" is the mark of this
contortion.

Gayatri Spivak

F, AS VALERY SUGGESTED, "a poem is never finished, it
is only abandoned," then authorial manuscripts — even
more than their printed counterparts — should provide us
with the materials for a poetics of abandonment. Such a poetics
would be based, of course, on a principle of imperfection, on
the knowledge that even the greatest poems are willfully (or
reluctantly) abandoned by their authors to the public, passed as

When Rodney Dennis retired as our distinguished Curator of Manuscripts
at the Houghton Library in 1992 (our fiftieth anniversary year), he asked several of us to join him in writing short critical essays about interesting manuscripts in our collection. Rodney parceled the manuscripts out to us, and
we accepted his invitation — which was also a challenge — with alacrity.
This essay first appeared with the Spartan title "Alexander Pope, *An Essay on
Man*, Epistles I-III" in *The Marks in the Fields: Essays on the Uses of Manuscripts*, edited by Rodney G. Dennis with Elizabeth Falsey (Cambridge MA:
The Houghton Library, 1992), pp. 47-57.

fresh currency in the literary marketplace before they could be even more finely wrought. And of revision, polishing, and embellishment there is no end, unless author and text alike are to become rotten with perfection.

No one in English has written poems more finely nor drawn such incessant attention to the niceties of his craft than the enigmatic figure who translated the roughshod Homer for his eighteenth-century audience:

Be *Homer's* Works your *Study*, and *Delight*,
Read them by Day, and meditate by Night,
Thence form your Judgment, thence your Maxims bring,
And trace the Muses *upward* to their *Spring*.

And yet Pope, of all people, discloses an unusual ambivalence in his strategies of textual abandonment. Take, for example, the opening epistle of *An Essay on Man*, which Pope delivered to the public in late February of 1733. Rarely has a poem of such disarming ambition been published in such a tentative way. Pope "Address'd" the poem "to a FRIEND," but did not name him. He stipulated that this was merely "PART I," thus signaling that more text (and more expense) would follow. He not only published the epistle anonymously, but went out of his way to convince his readers that he was not the poem's author: "*As he imitates no Man, so he would be thought to vye with no Man in these Epistles, particularly with the noted Author of* TWO lately published" (the "Epistle to Bathurst" and "The First Satire of the Second Book of Horace," both of which bore Pope's name). It was also his practice to purchase several copies of his newly published poems so that he could mark them up for later editions. It should therefore not surprise us that only three months later he would issue the text again, "Corrected by the AUTHOR," only to supersede it the following year when the four epistles were published in a corrected, collected edition that still failed to proclaim Pope's authorship but did include the formal dedication to Bolingbroke.

It might therefore be prudent to say that Pope did not abandon his poems so much as *launch* them: delivering them to the public without, at least at first, benefit of authorial protection; carefully gauging their progress in the coffeehouses and the press; correcting, revising, and amplifying them as epistle followed epistle; and then collecting them in a standard edition that itself would take different forms (folio, quarto, octavo) and eventually be superseded by later collections, with the text continuing to be fine-tuned even for the so-called "death-bed edition" compiled by Warburton. Important substantive changes were introduced at several stages in the chain of textual transmission, but no detail was too small to be neglected. Pope tinkered assiduously with punctuation, capitalization (including small caps), the spacing as well as the precise sequence of verse paragraphs, the ornaments, initial letters, and introductory material, the frontispiece, and especially the play between roman and italic, preferring a consciously simple, unadorned, roman style for the collected editions, but providing helpful italics for the readers of his popular editions. A poem by Pope, in other words, may have been easily — if carefully and cunningly — abandoned into print, but it finally escaped the authorial imprint of its progenitor only with the poet's death.

Pope's manuscripts tell an even more complicated tale. Two holographs of *An Essay on Man* have survived; both were at one time in the possession of Jonathan Richardson the Younger, to whom Pope presented all of his papers "for the pains I [Richardson] took in collating the whole with the printed editions, at his request, on my having proposed to him the 'making

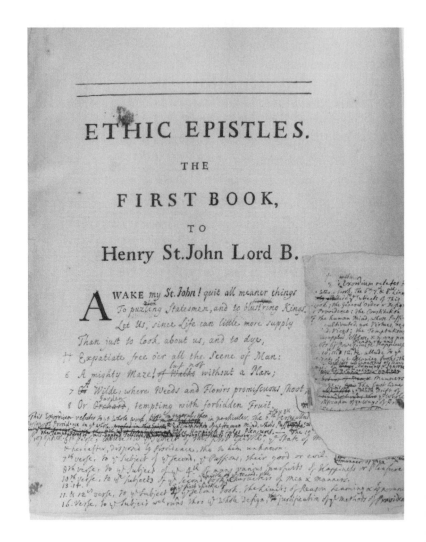

FIGURE 7.
Alexander Pope, *An Essay on Man*, autograph manuscript (1731).
By permission of The Houghton Library, Harvard College Library.

an edition of his works in the manner of Boileau's.'" The earlier of the two manuscripts, now at the Pierpont Morgan Library, actually contains all four of the completed poem's epistles, whereas the Houghton manuscript, which may date from the summer of 1731, contains only the first three. It is generally agreed that the Houghton manuscript began as a fair copy of the Morgan manuscript before the fourth epistle was begun (we know that Pope often produced such fair copies for his friends, only to begin treating them as alternative working copies soon afterwards). On the first page of text in the Houghton manuscript (figure 7), we encounter, for instance, not only a full title and dedication — both lacking in Morgan — but also an example of Pope's formal, "print" hand actually imitating the letters and rules of a typeset edition. This marvelously fine, spidery hand fills both manuscripts. Pope's informal hand (much rougher, larger, and angular) is rarely to be found, although both holographs include numerous revisions and additions that betray some of the heat of composition, particularly in the marginal commentaries on the poem.

Generally speaking, the Morgan manuscript is more heavily reworked than Houghton's, especially the fourth epistle, which Maynard Mack describes as "the roughest of all Pope's surviving working papers"; but many of the more extensive (and permanent) revisions occur in Houghton, and some — not surprisingly — occur in both. The text of the first edition (1733a) follows neither manuscript exactly, nor would we expect it to; the uncertainty of both holographs suggests that there must have been yet another working copy that reconciled these two and, beyond that, perhaps a fair copy for the printer as well. This is certainly borne out by the rest of Richardson's commentary: "As for his *Essay on Man,* ... I was witness to the whole conduct of it in writing, and actually have his original MSS. for it from the first scratches of the four books, to the several finished copies (of his own neat and elegant writing these last)." What is certain, however, is Pope's reluctance to abandon earlier, rougher, less visually pleasing drafts, even after the poem had been launched into print. (Nor, for that matter, did he completely abandon the textual variants themselves after the printed poem had appeared: the 1736 collected edition of his works included variants in the manner of a classical text!) Two examples from the opening of the poem pose some of the complications. Consider, in the first place, the poet's invocation of his friend Bolingbroke:

> *Morgan:* Awake my Memmius, leave all meaner things
> *Houghton:* Awake my St. John! quit all meaner things
> *1733a:* AWAKE! my Lælius, leave all meaner Things
> *1733b:* AWAKE! my Lælius, leave all meaner Things
> *1734:* Awake! my St. John! leave all meaner things

Here we can see Pope moving initially from the classical and anonymous Memmius of the Morgan manuscript to the honest and familiar St. John of the Houghton copy, which also substitutes "quit" for "leave." Neither change, it should be noted, emerges at the expense of a deletion; both were fresh (but mature) thoughts *before* Pope wrote out what appears, at first, to have been a fair copy. By the time the first epistle was published (1733a), Pope had decided to return to "leave" and to choose a more formal name for Bolingbroke — but not the Memmius of the Morgan manuscript. The second edition that followed a few months later (1733b) included no changes in the opening line, but a year later, having now dedicated the four-epistle poem to Bolingbroke, Pope reverted to the St. John of the Houghton manuscript and stayed with it until he died.

The sixth, seventh, and eighth lines disclose a textual transmission that is almost as convoluted — and much more famous — as Pope invites us to join him in examining the *"Scene of Man"*:

Morgan:
  A mighty *Maze!* of *Walks* without a Plan;
  Or *Wilde,* where Weeds and Flowrs promiscuous shoot;
  Or *Orchard,* tempting with forbidden Fruit.
Houghton:
  A Mighty Maze! but not without a Plan;
  A Wilde, where Weeds and Flow'rs promiscuous shoot;
  Or Garden, tempting with forbidden Fruit.
1733a:
  A mighty Maze! of walks without a Plan;
  Or Wild, where weeds and flow'rs promiscuous shoot;
  Or Garden, tempting with forbidden fruit.
1733b
  A mighty Maze! but not without a Plan;
  A Wilde, where weeds and flowers promiscuous shoot,
  Or Garden, tempting with forbidden fruit.

In this collation we see that all three variants which emerge in the Houghton manuscript are interlineations that suppress a cancelled original, and this naturally suggests that they were afterthoughts made following the publication of the first edition, which follows the Morgan text. But this is not true of Pope's transition from an *"Orchard"* to a "Garden" within the Houghton manuscript, for "Garden" was printed in the *first* edition. The ink, the hand, and the method of insertion are identical here to the examples in the previous two lines, even though it is logical to conclude that those changes were made at a slightly later date.

Uncertainties and ambiguities such as these are the stock-in-trade of both the Morgan and the Houghton manuscripts, and it is unlikely whether the precise relationship of the two holographs to each other — and to the early printings — will ever be completely gauged without recourse to even more manuscript material. If we are faced with an embarrassment of riches, it is only because the generation and makeover of Pope's works are so unrelentingly complicated that we continually aspire to possess *all* of the poetical documents that the author presented to the younger Richardson. Even working within these inevitable restraints, however, scholars have been able to put the two surviving manuscripts to remarkably good use. Mack has demonstrated how the progress from Morgan to Houghton to the first edition discloses the development of a more serious decorum in the poem that can be glimpsed in its increased gravity and abstraction. "But the right decorum did not reveal itself to the poet in a flash," Mack cautiously warns: "it was painfully won." Miriam Leranbaum has carefully examined the manuscripts in her effort to chart the relationship between *An Essay on Man* and the ambitious but never completed *Opus Magnum* of which it was to form the first part. And David Foxon, who has scrutinized both the manuscripts and the early printings of this and other poems by Pope with an unusual eye for the telling detail, has been able to suggest just how closely the poet worked for (and with) his printers, and how carefully he prepared his texts with both their immediate *and* their later editions in mind. For a comparable example of such extraordinary forethought one would have to turn to Hogarth's practice of executing his paintings in reverse so that the inverted engravings later taken from them would possess the image the artist originally had in mind and ultimately wished to disseminate.

But the problems and ambiguities persist, and justifiably so in a philosophical poem that marked a new turning in the author's career. Critical fervor has been most heated, moreover, whenever it has focused on the revision in the sixth line that instructed Pope's readers to envision "the *Scene of Man*" not as a mighty maze "of *Walks* without a Plan," which was the reading in the Morgan manuscript and the first printing (1733a), but rather as a mighty maze that is "not without a Plan," the interlinear reading in the Houghton copy and in the second (and all subsequent) editions. But how significant, precisely, is the difference between these two variants? Most criticism has in fact tended to explain any distinction away. In his *Life of Pope*, Samuel Johnson — who was no great admirer of this particular poem — bluntly concluded that the poet made this change because, "if there were no plan, it was in vain to describe or to trace the maze." A. D. Nuttall is in agreement: "It is sometimes thought that this change shows how far Pope's mind was from serious theology, since he could switch in a moment from a planless (Godless) universe to a God-directed one. But the earlier version need only imply that we do not possess the plan of the maze."

The young William Empson struck a similar note, arguing that the two lines "are very nearly the same; a *maze* is conceived as something that at once has and has not got a *plan*" in the sense that "it was designed with a *plan* to start with, but the *plan* has since been lost, or at any rate is not being shown to you." This is a level-headed conclusion, especially considering that it derives from a citation of the poem ("A mighty maze, and all without a plan") that neither the Morgan nor the Houghton manuscript can support! And it has essentially been corroborated by Mack, who points out that there is both intricacy and plan in either reading: the first emphasizes the fact that man does not have a chart (or drawing, or sketch) of the maze; the second stresses the fact that there is order in the maze ("plan" here signifying a scheme of arrangement), even though man can obtain only glimmerings of its nature. Mack had recourse to the OED to support his distinctions, but the language he invoked had already been broached by Pope in the "Design" to the collected edition of 1734:

> *What is now published, is only to be considered as a general Map of* MAN, *marking out no more than the* Greater Parts, *their* Extent, *their* Limits, *and their* Connection, *but leaving the Particular to be more fully delineated in the Charts which are to follow,*

by which Pope meant the moral epistles and presumably the unfinished poems that were to complete his *Opus Magnum.*

Each of these explanations is reasonable, and yet none tells us why Pope made such a change, nor what the revision does to the larger poetical passage in which it occurs. Let us begin, then, with the maze itself.

A maze is, above all else, a profoundly paradoxical structure. It is manmade, artful, and (because it partakes of natural elements) artificial. A maze makes nature appear to be orderly, but in fact provides more difficulty and mischance than we normally find in nature itself. On the one hand, it tames nature, cultivating — or at least embellishing — the landscape; on the other hand, it intentionally bewilders those who would attempt to penetrate its mysteries. It places natural and human, tame and wild elements in a deliberate tension. By bewildering us, moreover, it figuratively (and paradoxically) places us once again in the wild. As Pope put it in the *Essay on Criticism,*

Some are bewilder'd in the Maze of Schools,
And some made *Coxcombs* Nature meant but *Fools.*

Mazes can most easily be analyzed from above (and thus we are asked to "Expatiate free, o'er *all* the *Scene of Man*"), but can only be experienced from below. The maze is, in short, a remarkably rich metaphor that figures the complexity Pope attributed to the human condition.

By specifying that this is a mighty maze "of *Walks* without a Plan," Pope is simply expanding upon the central contradiction that is compressed in the figure of the maze itself. The very fact that there are "*Walks*" signals the presence of design and agency; the italics and capitalization within the Morgan manuscript, moreover, visually reinforce the importance and formality of Pope's expanded metaphor. The maze tempts us to enter, but we have not been provided with a plan (a map, a chart) that will show us how to proceed; and we therefore lack both direction and a sense of security.

The richness of the figure, however, is complicated by Pope's desire that we see the maze in two ways at once. Like so much eighteenth-century verse, *An Essay on Man* is a prospect poem, and our difficulty lies in establishing a perspective or point of view. The invitation Pope extends to us to move freely "o'er" the scene of man prepares us to view the maze from above, whereas the transition to its walks and to the missing plan of its design firmly returns us to our normal, terrestrial perspective (as do the metaphorical "*Wilde*" and "*Orchard*" or "Garden" that follow). It is difficult to invoke the language of the senses to describe metaphysical matters but, as Pope discovered in the course of writing his most abstract and philosophical poem, it is the only language we have. In the margins of the manuscripts (and often in the explanations that were appended to the printed texts), Pope could strive toward an even plainer idiom. As the note beneath the exordium on the first page of the Houghton manuscript states, "ye State of Man

[is] disposed by Providence, tho to him [to man] unknown."
Or as the muscular lines of the first epistle's conclusion protest
(perhaps too loudly),

> All Nature is but Art, unknown to thee;
> All Chance, Direction which thou canst not see;
> All Discord, Harmony not understood;
> All partial Evil, universal Good. [1734]

Each of these terms and each of these paradoxes is closely associated with the figure of the maze — even though they are separated from one another by almost 300 lines of verse — but the
tension between nature and art is the most telling, for it values
art above nature and equates what is artful with what is divine.

The eventual shift in the Houghton manuscript and in later
printings of the poem to "A mighty Maze! but not without a
Plan" marks more than a mere refinement of Pope's original
reading. In the original line, the second half extends and
explains the first; in the revised line, however, the second half is
set in opposition rather than apposition to the first ("but not
without") in a gesture of reassurance. The revision replaces
both the logic of the maze and the structure of the poetical
argument. If we understand what a maze is, then why do we
need to be told there is a design? The only question is whether
we will be able to reach the center of the labyrinth, or — to
quote from the argument of the poem added in 1734 — view the
"NATURE and STATE of MAN, with respect to the UNIVERSE." As
Nuttall remarked, "the earlier version need only imply that we
do not possess the plan of the maze," and I would argue that it
is clearly the weakness of mere implication alone that troubled
Pope as he moved in the second half of the line to an explicit
statement concerning providential agency. I think it is entirely

likely that, in the months following the initial publication of the first epistle, Pope discovered that his readers needed to be given specific directions so that the poem itself did not become an ambiguous and bewildering maze.

What, then, are we to make of the "*Wilde*" of the seventh line and the "*Orchard*" or "Garden" of the eighth? Both lines offer us fresh ways of visualizing, through the language of sense, the "mixed" condition that is the "*Scene of Man.*" In the wild, "Weeds and Flowrs promiscuous shoot": here the setting is entirely natural and uncultivated, but the second half of the line necessarily privileges the flowers that are worth cultivating, and underscores the illicit mixing of the two. ("Passions are cultivated or neglected," as Pope's marginal gloss on this line in the Houghton manuscript points out.) The figure of the orchard returns us to the artful nature of the maze, tempting us to enter its exotic domain. The revision in the Houghton manuscript to "Garden" reinforces the Miltonic allusion and domesticates the natural figure even more than a maze does. Here we find an entirely cultivated nature that is *open* to view, even if what it offers is both unfamiliar and forbidden to us. The "*Wilde*" and "Garden" do not modify the maze; they offer us alternative ways of thinking about the scene of man. But together they contain the elements of the maze — a bewildering garden that tempts the beholder to enter — and like the maze they combine the natural and the artful, what is wild and what is cultivated (weeds and flowers, forbidden fruit).

The revisions in the Houghton manuscript should therefore be seen as part of a careful process of domestication (and reassurance) in the opening lines of the poem. They reinforce the reader's sense of human agency and providential order. Pope's need to tinker with his original text, moreover, betrays his difficulty in writing philosophical verse by naturalizing religion (or, at the very least, it betrays his concern for the progress of his readers). Do these surviving variants also provide a record of the poet working through his own argument? Were the marginal plans and commentaries and exordia meant to help *him* as well as us? Was he as struck as we are by his disclaimer in the "Design" that "*There are not* many certain Truths *in this World*"? Possessing no answers to these questions, we may join Mack in finding what in his "own experience has proved true of poetical manuscripts generally, no matter whose — that they cast little light on the questions of greatest interest."

Poetical manuscripts do, however, inevitably change the way we read the poems they become. Our view of an entire manuscript, or of the transition between one and another, or of the larger chain of textual transmission once the poem has been printed provides us with an extended view of the poet's creative process: a perspective above as well as within the maze. By showing us the alternatives, these manuscripts visually remind us that, no matter how polished and finely wrought the poetical icon may become, texts actually evolve as decisions are slowly and sometimes haltingly made. Textual variants, moreover, enable us to argue with a writer in his or her own terms. What may have been abandoned in printed editions — even in critical editions as elaborate as the Twickenham Pope — remain as pentimenti in the manuscript. It is language *sous rature*: not precisely in the Derridean sense, for textual variants are eventually *displaced* rather than simply crossed through or placed "under erasure." But it is nonetheless language that has been claimed, decided against because of its inadequacy, but never entirely abandoned to obscurity so long as these manuscripts survive and scholars continue to be sucked into their vortex.

Readers of manuscripts are no longer innocent readers. Variants inevitably condition our response to a poem or to a particular passage. The phrase "of *Walks* without a Plan" would surely seem less ominous — might, indeed, appear to be perfectly logical — if it had no successor. The line "A Mighty Maze! but not without a Plan" would certainly read differently today if we did not know what had preceded it. And the very fact that I can argue with Pope is based on the evidence we have that Pope argued with himself. My own view is that the revision in the sixth line, while it may have been necessary for Pope's readers, both dissipates the power of the paradox that is figured by the maze and disrupts the strategy by which each introductory metaphor in these three lines is extended (rather than modified) in the words that follow. For Pope (no less than for Derrida) our very language is twisted and bent even as it guides us. But the more important point is that, whether or not the variant here improves or maims the text, the change itself (which speaks so emphatically) actually reflects the tentativeness of the poem. Balance, antithesis, and linguistic tension are crucial throughout the poem. Surely the emendation here is too final, too affirmative, too lapidary for an opening stanza: its self-assurance has not yet been earned.

Perhaps only the language of paradox and contradiction is appropriate to a description of human nature: not just in these few lines but in the many etched passages that follow, and particularly, of course, in the beginning of the second epistle with its rich Shakespearean echoes:

Plac'd on this Isthmus of a middle state,
A Being darkly wise, and rudely great;
With too much Knowledge for the Sceptic side,
With too much weakness for a Stoic's pride,
He hangs between; in doubt to act, or rest,
In doubt to deem himself a God, or Beast,

In doubt his mind or body to prefer,
Born but to die, and reas'ning but to err;
Alike in ignorance, his Reason such,
Whether he thinks too little, or too much.
Chaos of Thought and Passion, all confus'd;
Still by himself abus'd, or dis-abus'd;
Created half to rise, and half to fall;
Great Lord of all things, yet a Prey to all;
Sole Judge of Truth, in endless Error hurl'd,
The Glory, Jest, and Riddle of the world! [1734]

Perhaps we can only augment the paradoxical vision of the *Essay* by turning to Burke — to *our* Burke, Kenneth — for a definition of man that specifically takes account of the double-edged nature of the language we wield:

Man is the symbol-using (symbol-making, symbol-misusing) animal, inventor of the negative (or moralized by the negative), separated from his natural condition by instruments of his own making, goaded by the spirit of hierarchy (or moved by the sense of order), and rotten with perfection.

SOURCES

Burke, Kenneth. *Language as Symbolic Action.* Berkeley: Univ. of California Press, 1966.
Butt, John. "Pope's Poetical Manuscripts." *Proceedings of the British Academy* 40 (1954): 23-39.
Derrida, Jacques. *Of Grammatology.* Trans. Gayatri Chakravorty Spivak. Baltimore: The Johns Hopkins Univ. Press, 1974.

Empson, William. *Seven Types of Ambiguity.* London: Chatto and Windus, 1930.

Foxon, David. *Pope and the Early Eighteenth-Century Book Trade.* Rev. and ed. James McLaverty. The Lyell Lectures, Oxford, 1975-1976. Oxford: Clarendon Press, 1991.

Johnson, Samuel. *Lives of the English Poets.* Ed. George Birkbeck Hill. 3 vols. Oxford: Clarendon Press, 1905.

Leranbaum, Miriam. *Alexander Pope's 'Opus Magnum' 1729-1744.* Oxford: Clarendon Press, 1977.

Mack, Maynard. " 'The Last and Greatest Art': Pope's Poetical Manuscripts." In *Collected in Himself: Essays Critical, Biographical, and Bibliographical on Pope and Some of His Contemporaries.* Newark: Univ. of Delaware Press; London and Toronto: Associated University Presses, 1982, pp. 322-347.

_____, ed. *The Last and Greatest Art: Some Unpublished Poetical Manuscripts of Alexander Pope.* Newark: Univ. of Delaware Press; London and Toronto: Associated University Presses, 1984.

Morris, David B. *Alexander Pope: The Genius of Sense.* Cambridge MA: Harvard Univ. Press, 1984.

Nuttall, A. D. *Pope's "Essay on Man."* London: Allen and Unwin, 1984.

Pope, Alexander. *An Essay on Man.* Ed. Maynard Mack. Vol. 3, Pt. 1 of the Twickenham edn. of *The Poems of Alexander Pope.* New Haven: Yale Univ. Press, London: Methuen, 1950.

_____. *An Essay on Man: Reproductions of the Manuscripts in the Pierpont Morgan Library and the Houghton Library with the Printed Text of the Original Edition.* Introd. Maynard Mack. Oxford: Roxburghe Club, 1962.

Sherburn, George. "Pope at Work." In *Essays on the Eighteenth Century Presented to David Nichol Smith in honour of his seventieth birthday.* Oxford: Clarendon Press, 1945, pp. 49-64.

Chapter 5
Piranesi's Double Ruin

P ERHAPS IT IS in the very nature of Rome to be read as
a palimpsest, as the site of perpetual double-exposure.[1]
Throughout the centuries, the modern eye finds its vision
of the eternal city constantly undermined by — and therefore
superimposed upon — visual reminders of a monumental past,
a past so present that contemporary sensibility must accommodate rather than attempt to obliterate it. In November 1786, during his very first days in Rome, Goethe noted that "I find it a
difficult and melancholy business, I must confess, separating the
old Rome from the new."[2] In the stillness of an autumnal
evening two decades earlier, the historian Edward Gibbon found
in the juxtaposition of the old and the new not only the inspira-
tion for, but also the central thesis of what would become his
magnum opus. Here is how he recalled that moment years later
in one of the six versions of his memoirs:

The impetus for this essay, as I noted in Chapter 3, was the publication of
Andrew Robison's catalogue of Piranesi's architectural fantasies in 1986, an
event that opened my eyes to the alterations the artist had made to his earliest work as a printmaker. This essay first appeared in *Eighteenth-Century
Studies* 34 (2000): 161-180 and then as Boston Athenæum Occasional Paper
No. 2, without footnotes but with a preface describing the Athenæum's collection of Piranesi's etchings.

In my Journal the place and moment of conception are recorded; the fifteenth of October 1764, in the close of evening, as I sat musing in the Church of the Zoccolanti or Franciscan fryars, while they were singing Vespers in the Temple of Jupiter on the ruins of the Capitol.[3]

Gibbons's great historical project was originally "circumscribed to the decay of the City," he notes, but it soon extended to the Empire itself.

No one is more closely associated with this double vision of ancient and contemporary Rome than Giovanni Battista Piranesi, the Venetian-born printmaker and sometime architect in whose "strange linear universe," as Marguerite Yourcenar has nicely phrased it, "all the eighteenth-century angles of incidence and reflection intersect."[4] Piranesi's views of Rome had such a profound influence on the cultural imagination of the late eighteenth century, in fact, that the images themselves became yet another superimposition with which the modern eye would have to contend. Writing in his *Italian Journey*, Goethe confessed that his first sight of the ruins of Rome had failed to measure up to Piranesi's views of them,[5] and Horace Walpole urged his contemporaries to "study the sublime dreams of Piranesi, who seems to have conceived visions of Rome beyond what it boasted even in the meridian of its splendor":

Savage as Salvator Rosa, fierce as Michael Angelo, and exuberant as Rubens, he has imagined scenes that would startle geometry, and exhaust the Indies to realize. He piles palaces on bridges, and temples on palaces, and scales heaven with mountains of edifices. Yet what taste in his boldness! What grandeur in his wildness! what labour and thought both in his rashness and details![6]

If we look closely at Piranesi's first published book, the *Prima Parte di Architteture, e Prospettive* of 1743, we discover that the aspiring architect, then literally scraping together a living as an engraver in Rome, also found his early encounter with the ancient city to be a transforming experience, one that significantly shaped his highly personal work as an architect, etcher, and designer. The sheer virtuosity of the thirteen etchings in this volume is matched only by Piranesi's learning and bravado. Both of his modern editors, Andrew Robison and John Wilton-Ely, agree that it is a truly extraordinary collection of prints, a publication that demonstrates how quickly and deeply the young artist had absorbed and in many ways transcended the graphic *and* architectural models available to him during the early 1740s.[7] It is also, I argue, a remarkably proleptic event in Piranesi's long and contentious career, revealing not just his growing mastery of subject and style, but the beginning, as well, of his lifelong attempt to inscribe order — legibility — on what remained of the Roman past. My focus in this essay is therefore trained on the fate of writing within these early prints, and — most importantly — on the affinity Piranesi sensed so early in his career between the medium of etching and the nature of the ruins he depicted. Beginning with the title-page of his first publication, Piranesi began to question not just the intelligibility of the past, but the stability of his own artistic explorations. Piranesi's *œuvre* as a whole might be said to manifest a strong confidence that the highest expression of the engraver's art could successfully be combined with abundant and fully legible writing; a close examination of his first publication suggests, however, that such confidence was not easily won.

In the dedicatory pages of the *Prima Parte*, Piranesi wrote that "These speaking ruins have filled my spirit with images that accurate drawings, even such as those of the immortal Palladio, could never have succeeded in conveying, though I always kept them before my eyes."[8] This would be an extraordinary statement even if it did not come from an immodest, twenty-three-year-old *arriviste* attempting — again, literally — to place his mark on what he hoped would become his adopted city. Even the Palladian forms with which he was so familiar in his native Venice, he argues, cannot convey the images that have filled his spirit, images inspired by the ruins he has directly beheld. But of what, precisely, do these eloquent ruins speak? The implicit answer in Piranesi's formulation is a vision of monumental Rome in what Walpole called "the meridian of its splendor," a vision imprinted on the sensibility of only the most ambitious, daring, and sensitive modern artist.

Like aspiring architects before him, Piranesi must constantly experience a form of double vision in which a grand, reconstructive view of Rome is superimposed on the surviving fragments of its ancient past. Also implicit in Piranesi's polemical formulation is the no less important contrast between the architectural monuments of the past and the comparatively unimaginative achievements of contemporary Roman architects. (Or, to put his argument in a more precise historical context, as Piranesi himself does elsewhere, the comparatively meager financial market for innovative architecture in the Rome of the early 1740s.) "Therefore," he continues in his dedicatory pages, "having the idea of presenting to the world some of these images, but not hoping for an architect of these times who could effectively execute some of them . . . there seems to be no recourse than for me or some other modern architect to explain his ideas through his drawings."[9]

Explaining one's architectural ambitions through one's drawings (or etchings) is certainly not an unusual situation; it is, if anything, the predicament of the aspiring or out-of-work architect of any period. A treatise of the "first part" of architecture and perspective appearing in 1743, moreover, could be expected to share close affinities with a publication such as the architect and scene-designer Giuseppe Bibiena's *Architteture e Prospettive* of 1740 (and the similarities between these two remarkable books have frequently been noted).[10] What *is* unusual in Piranesi's first quire of published etchings, however — apart from the self-aggrandizing timbre of the dedication, which was also surely meant to stimulate his more cautious colleagues — is the imaginative reach of the plates themselves, thirteen of them in the first issue of the first edition.

Most of the plates represent buildings that are in relatively complete condition. Some of these buildings are modern in design and appear to be influenced by Bibiena: we can see this most clearly in the baroque configuration of the *Galleria grande di Statue* or in the more gothic interior of the *Carcere oscura* (figure 8), which has often been considered a harbinger of the great *carceri* series later in the decade.[11] Other "intact" buildings are consciously antique and bear titles such as *Mausoleo antico*, *Atrio Dorico*, or *Sala all'uso degli antichi Romani*. In each case, whether the edifice be ancient or more-or-less modern, the building is imaginary and the setting is contemporary (note, for instance, that each building is visited or inhabited by Roman figures of the eighteenth century).

One of the most beautiful of these etchings, the silvery *Campidoglio antico* (figure 9), which clearly anticipates the enormously successful *vedute* that established Piranesi's reputation later in the decade, was entitled *Forma ideale del Campidoglio antico* in the first issue (but never afterwards). Surely

FIGURE 8.
Giovanni Battista Piranesi, *Carcere oscura*, etching, from the *Prima Parte* (1743). By permission of the Department of Printing and Graphic Arts, The Houghton Library, Harvard College Library.

FIGURE 9.
Giovanni Battista Piranesi, *Campidoglio antico*, etching, from the *Prima
Parte* (1743). By permission of the Department of Printing and Graphic
Arts, The Houghton Library, Harvard College Library.

the antecedent was unnecessary, for each of the designs was,
by definition, an ideal form inspired by the past. The buildings
Piranesi offered his public were not, strictly speaking, replicas
or precise reconstructions of other structures, although he
would spend much of the rest of his career documenting what
remained of this Roman legacy. What he offered, rather, were
contemporary conceptions that, while they may be inspired by
— and blend in harmoniously with — older edifices, would
stake out their own claim to monumentality in the Rome of
the 1740s. These new but appropriately monumental conceptions have produced the "images" that have filled his "spirit,"
the "ideas" that can be "explained" only through the medium
of etching and engraving. Piranesi saw no abrupt break

between past and present, but rather a salutary continuum —
and this is why the ancient stones continue to speak to him.

Two of the original thirteen plates of the *Prima Parte*, on the
other hand, depict buildings or scenes that are currently in ruin;
these too, it must be emphasized, are also imaginary constructions, not documentary records of existing sites. The first of
these images is the volume's illustrated title-page (figure 10),
which serves as the principal focus of this essay. The second is
the *Rovine d'antichi Edifizj* (figure 11), arguably the first etching
in which Piranesi introduces what will soon become one of his
most characteristic motifs: an arrangement of contemporary
figures attempting to make sense of the ancient ruins and
inscriptions they have inherited, prototypes — so to speak — of
the Goethes and Gibbons who would inevitably follow.

It is important that we reconcile (or at least compare) these
two images of ruins with the preponderance of plates devoted
to buildings that are shown to be in relatively good repair. The
eleven plates depicting rooms, prisons, staircases, atria, mau-
soleums, or bridges that are still intact draw upon ancient and
baroque sources but translate them into designs for contemporary use (this, at least, is Piranesi's conceit). The two plates
depicting ruins, on the other hand, are predicated on the conception of an ancient building or site that has deteriorated with
time; and this is essentially a double act of the imagination, for
neither the "original" model nor the "surviving" ruin actually
existed. All of the plates of the *Prima Parte* appear to have a documentary flavor, but none so much as the two *capricci*, which
stand, paradoxically, two removes from any possible source.

Given Piranesi's explicit aim in his dedicatory text, the inclusion of *any* plates devoted to ruins within the *Prima Parte* is, at
first glance, an odd choice for an aspiring architect to make. The
juxtaposition of crumbling and intact buildings certainly

FIGURE 10.
Giovanni Battista Piranesi, title-page (first state) to the *Prima Parte*, etching (1743).
By permission of the Department of Printing and Graphic Arts, The Houghton
Library, Harvard College Library.

FIGURE 11.
Giovanni Battista Piranesi, *Rovine d'antichi Edifizj*, etching, from the *Prima Parte* (1743). By permission of the Department of Printing and Graphic Arts, The Houghton Library, Harvard College Library.

demonstrates the young artist's virtuosity and antiquarian interests, but it does so with more bravura than practicality. When Piranesi issued revised sets of the prints later in the decade, moreover, he chose to introduce only two additional prints of intact buildings (the *Gruppo di Colonne* and the *Tempio antico*) whereas he devoted three new etchings to buildings in ruin: *Vestiggi d'antichi Edificj, Ara antica,* and the *Camera sepolcrale.* He also continued to revise the *Rovine d'antichi Edifizj,* issuing it in numerous states over the years as *Ruine di Sepolcro antico.* These additional plates either closely anticipate or are coterminous with Piranesi's execution of his early *vedute,* the first states of his *carceri,* and the *grotteschi,* the prints by which he was — and still remains — best known. They suggest, moreover, that his increasingly intense focus on the depiction of ruins was particularly suited to the etching process, even when it was augmented by engraving, drypoint, and scraping, as it often was in these early plates.[12] The process of etching, in which the artist draws with a stylus on the copperplate's varnished surface (rather than working with an engraving burin *into* the copper itself), allows the acid to produce soft, delicate, spidery, even painterly effects with the printer's ink.

Some of this heightened mastery of technique can be seen in the often subtle changes Piranesi introduced in the second state of the title-page at the end of 1743 or beginning of 1744 (figure 12). Except for the obvious change in the dedicatory title itself, the two plates look remarkably alike: there are no alterations in the principal elements of the original title plate, only microscopic changes in the way in which Piranesi reworks or introduces objects with a delicate, almost feather-like technique. Andrew Robison points in particular to the deft and sophisticated way in which the foliage at the bottom center of the plate is executed in the revised state.[13] But much of the copperplate

FIGURE 12.
Giovanni Battista Piranesi, title-page (second state) to the *Prima Parte* (1743-44). By permission of the Department of Printing and Graphic Arts, The Houghton Library, Harvard College Library.

has actually been carefully reworked, including the marble tablet on which the title and dedication are carved.

Piranesi's conception of the title-page as a collection of imaginary Roman antiquities — some in ruin, some more or less preserved, as in the *veduta ideata* of Panini[14] — is an intriguing conceit, visually embodying what it verbally proclaims, and thus providing a symbolic introduction to the bifurcated series of plates that follows. This unusual strategy means, however, that the title itself cannot stand at center stage. Consigned to the right-hand side of the print, placed at a recess in the middle distance, and inscribed on a reclining slab of partially overgrown marble, Piranesi's title imposes at least a modest amount of visual exercise on the part of the reader. This labor increases slightly as one examines the revised second state, where the entire marble tablet — which reminds us, of course, of the copperplate on which the entire image has been etched — has been burnished clean and heavily reworked.[15] Piranesi augments his dedication to his mentor, the builder and connoisseur Nicola Giobbe, by including information about his own recent election to an artistic society, the Arcadi, that placed particular value on the symbolic forms that were emerging in these *capricci*.[16] But the major change here is not so much in the expansion of the text as in the style of the inscription, which has modulated from the large, dark, deeply "chiseled" lettering of the original plate to the comparatively light, shallow, and more evenly "carved" lettering of the revised plate a few months later.

I place "chiseled" and "carved" in quotation marks because both prints are etchings that represent marble which has been incised. The visual style of the first inscription, however, is that of the engraver, whereas the marble tablet of the revised plate begins to suggest the softness of the entire etching. This stylistic development can be seen most fully by the time the plate has reached its fourth state (the sixth issue of the first edition) in 1748, five years after its first publication. (There are minor alterations in the third state, but these are — to borrow a distinction from textual editing — accidental rather than substantive.) Piranesi's final rendering of the title-page (figure 3), which would remain intact throughout his lifetime, is dramatically different in almost every way from its two predecessors — in its style, its text, and even its subject — and it therefore provides us with a remarkable opportunity to chart the growth of the artist during some of the earliest moments of his career.

The most pervasive change to be found in this final version of Piranesi's title-page lies in the artist's handling of light. The play between the dark obelisk on the left side of the print and the more lightly modeled elements on the right began to appear in the second state, but by the fourth state the contrast in values has deepened into dramatic chiaroscuro. The temple in the far distance (at the top of the plate) and the marble tablet are now the focus of intense and radiant light, and this carefully controlled experiment in tonality reinforces the feathery effects of the etching process. In order to carry out such pervasive changes, Piranesi has had to burnish clean and then once again etch the upper two-thirds of the copperplate (virtually everything except the obelisk on the left and the various fragments in the lower right of the print). In doing so, he has shrouded the temple in the background in hazy mist, turned the large, decorated urn near the center of the plate into a ruin, changed (yet again) the style and text of the inscription, covered the bottom of it in heavy fog, and (in his most theatrical gesture) introduced human figures throughout the composition. These spidery characters made their original appearance in the *Rovine d'antichi Edifizj* of the first issue (figure 11); five years later we find them positioned throughout the image — in the temple, in the middle ground, atop the urn, and directly in front of the inscription itself.

Taken as a whole, this heavily reworked and reconceptualized image begins to suggest the complexities of Piranesi's greatest work, particularly his handling of "ruins already fifteen hundred years old," as Yourcenar describes them in her exploration of what she calls the "dark brain" of Piranesi:

> broken stone and crumbling brick; the collapsing vault that welcomes light's intrusion; the tunnel of dark rooms opening in the distance on daylight streaming through a broken wall; the overhanging plinth, suspended on the brink of its collapse, the great broken rhythm of aqueducts and colonnades; temples and basilicas lying open as though turned inside out by the depredations of time and of man, so that the interior has now become a kind of exterior, everywhere invaded by space like a ship by water.[17]

It is this world, a world of fragmentation and disrupted vision, that Piranesi moves so decisively towards in this complex image, which both proclaims the subject of the plates to follow and simultaneously places its title under erasure. What could have led Piranesi to have taken such an extraordinary step?

The nominal reason for the re-articulation of the title-page was surely the death of Nicola Giobbe in October 1748.[18] Giobbe had shared his collection of books and prints with the young artist and had introduced him to Salvi and Vanvitelli, Rome's most successful architects at the beginning of the decade. It was therefore both natural and expedient for Piranesi to dedicate his first book to his first patron, trusting that further support and a possible commission would follow, and acknowledging his debt to Giobbe's instruction. "You not only showed me piece by piece all of the most singular beauties of this kind, ancient and modern that can be found in Rome," he wrote in his dedicatory letter at the end of the volume, "but you have shown with the example of your excellent drawings how one can make praiseworthy use of the discoveries of our great predecessors in new forms."[19] Following Giobbe's death, however, the dedicatory portion of the title-page disappeared, concealed in the whirling mist and scrutinized in vain by the gesticulating figures.

Years later, following a bitter dispute with Lord Charlemont, Piranesi would once again remove a dedicatory inscription from the title-page of one of his publications (the *Antichità Romane* of 1756).[20] There is no documentary evidence, however, to suggest that Piranesi and Giobbe had a falling out, or that Piranesi had been seriously disappointed in his expectations; as he made clear in his dedicatory letter, after all, he planned to forsake Rome immediately following the publication of this volume.[21] Piranesi therefore had several possible choices before him: he could omit a dedicatee and move the inscription to the center of the tablet, he could change the dedication in order to memorialize Giobbe, or he could change the dedicatee altogether, hoping to engage the patronage of someone who would advance his work. Instead, he dropped the dedicatory letter at the end of the book but retained the space devoted to the original dedicatory lines near the bottom of the tablet, replacing the original inscription (which had been completely burnished away) with a swirl of clouds and thereby drawing attention to what was no longer there.

This would appear to be an extreme example of visual playfulness and/or obscurantism, made all the more apparent by the gesturing figure in the center of the plate, who draws his

Figure 13.
Detail of figure 3: Giovanni Battista Piranesi, title-page (fourth state) to
the *Prima Parte*, etching (1748 and after). Private collection.

companion's attention to the words that can no longer be seen. One legible trace does actually remain, however, and it is to this single letter — a fragile capital "E" directly to the left of the ram's head (figure 13) — rather than to the clouds themselves that Piranesi's figure points. The letter has been painstakingly reworked in this final version of the plate rather than simply salvaged from the second and third states. It shares a silvery softness with the rest of the newly inscribed letters, which are executed in such an unusually free manner that two of the capital "N"s are actually reversed.[22] In a moment, even the final letter of Giobbe's name will disappear. And thus what we witness here is not simply an acknowledgment of the mysterious language of these speaking ruins, but also a re-enactment of the temporal and physical forces that engender ruin in the first place. Even the luxuriant vegetation reminds us of the indifference of the natural world and its continuing role as a destructive agent.

We also witness, in this proleptic image, the birth of Piranesi's lifelong fascination with the physical properties of language. The *Prima Parte* opens with a title that is theatrically embedded in what would otherwise be an illustrated frontispiece, and the book closes not with a visual flourish but with a written, highly polemical dedication. By the time this slim volume was issued for the third and fourth times in 1747 and 1748, the ordinary woodcut chosen for the initial letter "S" of the dedication had been replaced by an elegant, undulating, historiated letter of Piranesi's own design. And in the three successive title-pages we see not just the etcher's growing mastery of his medium, but also his burgeoning interest in the nature of ancient inscriptions. This fascination with the language of monuments would eventually lead to the publication of his *Lapides Capitolini* in 1761 and to the development of what

Armando Petrucci has characterized as the freedom and inge-
nuity of the *littera piranesiana.* In Petrucci's view, Piranesi's
learned and muscular lettering embodies "the monumental
written city," and it does so just as the images of imposing buildings first conceptualized in the *Prima Parte* do, by moving
beyond an accurate reconstruction of the past to "a global ide-
alization" of what imperial Rome had once been.[23]

In the early prints devoted to ruins, however, writing would
take a different turn. As early as the *Rovine d'antichi Edifizj* of
the first issue in 1743 (figure 11) we discover — as Piranesi's figures do — a pervasive threat to the very intelligibility of the
past. In the one surviving inscription in this early plate we can
make out the imperial "SPQR," but the rest of the lettering has
almost been worn smooth. In the second and third states of this
etching (1748 and afterwards), a third pointing figure has been
added, but the inscription itself has virtually disappeared; the
letters "SPQR" have been burnished out, and only a few dis-
jointed letters remain. In the title-page, as we have seen, the lettering of the inscription has modulated, with each revision,
towards a lighter, less heavily carved style of "engraving." By the
time Piranesi has reached his final (and most sophisticated)
version in 1748, moreover, writing itself has begun to disappear.

With the diminution of language comes the simultaneous
appearance of human figures, mute spectators attempting to
make sense of the inscription that disappears before their very
eyes. Human presence, in other words, is coterminous with linguistic absence or dissolution. Or, to put it the other way round,
the disappearance of language, of the dedicatory lines devoted
to Nicola Giobbe — as time, in the guise of mist or cloud, works
its effects on marble and the writing inscribed upon it — this
disappearance of a full text points to the need for interpretive
gestures. The figures who people this plate are not the faintly

threatening beggars of the urban *vedute*,[24] but rather the embodiment of "gesticulating humanity" (in Wilton-Ely's useful phrase),[25] symbolic characters that literally point to Piranesi's central concerns. They remind us of Alberti's preference for "someone who admonishes and points out to us what is happening [in an *istoria*]; or beckons with his hand to see; . . . or shows some danger or marvellous thing there; or invites us to weep or to laugh together with them."[26] They therefore exercise what Claude Gandelman has called the "gesture of demonstration," a perlocutionary act in which enlightenment successors to the demonstrator of early Renaissance religious painting force us to follow the vector of their gaze and thus confront the puzzle of the fragmented inscription ourselves.[27]

The figure with the extended arm gestures towards Piranesi's original, dedicatory gesture. What he points to, however, is almost entirely obscured by the natural forces that swirl before him. Because he and his companion cannot read — or can no longer read — beneath the swirling mist, his gesture might be paraphrased as "Giobbe is no more." And here we are faced with two additional paradoxes. In the first place, it is unlikely that most of the spectators of this image would be familiar with the dedication to Giobbe in the earlier states. Only a small cadre of elite readers — the connoisseurs of the Arcadi, for example — would be able to link the surviving "E" with Giobbe's name. For everyone else, the letter would simply stand as a mysterious marker of what *cannot* be seen and interpreted.[28] As John Sparrow pointed out in another context, "to use an inscription in a picture so that its effectiveness depends upon its being in part invisible, and the significant word the word that is not seen, implies a degree of sophistication in the artist" that is consistent with the wittiness of the Baroque epigraphists.[29] A second paradox emerges as we realize that the absence or disappearance of language marks the origin of narrative: a tale of human decay, of the death of someone who had educated and encouraged Piranesi during his formative years, and a narrative of hermeneutic engagement as we explore what the artist clearly wished to emphasize as missing or incomplete.

Piranesi's fascination with the instability of the inscription is consistent with a thematic tendency in European epigraphy that was at least a century old by the early 1740s. Petrucci has summarized this development as a "tendency to obscure the meaning of the graphic sign, to treat it as elusive, ambiguous, and difficult to decipher, thereby portraying monumental writing as something remote, fascinating, and pompous, decipherable only through conscious and strenuous effort."[30] He describes seventeenth-century images in which "the act of deciphering has become the central focus of the scene," and his depiction of one painting in particular, the second version of Poussin's *Et in Arcadia Ego* (figure 14), also suggests the focus of both Piranesi's title-page and the *Rovine d'antichi Edifizj*: "The figures gathered round are pointing out the inscription to each other and seem to be engaged in an antiquarian discussion about its meaning, but as far as the viewer of the painting is concerned, the inscription is quite illegible."[31]

Petrucci's final point is debatable, but it is clear that — like Louis Marin and W.J.T. Mitchell — he sees the focus of Poussin's painting as the scene of interpretation. "The event here," Marin argues, "is the story of enunciation or of representation. What is represented is the very process of representation."[32] For Mitchell, the painting is "a representation of a representation"; it is a metapicture in which we glimpse the stages in "a process of encounter, apprehension, puzzlement, and discussion."[33] And what is true of Poussin in his mature work is surely worth remarking of Piranesi in his very earliest,

FIGURE 14.
Nicolas Poussin, *Et in Arcadia Ego (The Arcadian Shepherds)*, painting
(second version, 1635). By permission of the Musée du Louvre.

where a self-conscious focus on the process of interpretation
serves as the initial gesture of his volume.

For Piranesi, as for his precursors, the partial obliteration of
the sign makes it loom even larger, with the pentimenti of the
inscriptions suggesting both the fragile and incomplete remains
of antiquity and the absolute certainty of human decay. These
two corollaries are almost always found together, as in the
superfluous reminder Diderot addressed to Hubert Robert, the
ultimate *ruiniste*:

Monsieur Robert, don't you know why ruins give such
pleasure, independent of the variety of accidents they
reveal? I will tell you. . . . Everything dissolves, everything

perishes, everything passes; only the world remains, only time endures... What is my ephemeral existence compared to crumbling stone? ... I see the marble of tombs crumble into powder and I don't want to die![34]

Et in Arcadia ego: each of Piranesi's modern commentators has had to confront the moral sententia implicitly embedded in his work. The responses range from Nicholas Penny's focus on Piranesi's "didacticism" ("He found in his ruins the evidence of their original strength and so enhances our awareness of the forces needed to defeat such buildings")[35] to Robert Moore's claim that Piranesi is "a great tragic artist":

Piranesi, it seems to me, makes us feel the precariousness of civilization. The despoiled tombs, the naked and decaying stonework stripped of its marble, haunted by cadaverous beggars, stand witness to the grim idea that obsessed Pope in the last *Dunciad*.[36]

Only Marguerite Yourcenar has responded with ambivalence to the human element in these speaking ruins. Characterizing Piranesi as "the interpreter and virtually the inventor of Rome's tragic beauty,"[37] she nonetheless interprets his work as a meditation on the life and death of *forms*. His ruins do not "release a discourse on the grandeur and decadence of empires and the instability of human affairs, but rather a meditation on the duration or the slow erosion of things, on the opaque identity of the block continuing, within the monument, its long existence of stone *as stone*."[38] The human figures introduced into these images serve no thematic or ironic function, she argues; they simply serve to accentuate the height of the vaults and the depth of the perspective.[39]

This is certainly *not* the role of the human figures in the pages of the *Prima Parte*, where they serve as hermeneutic markers pointing — across the obscuring mist that hides virtually any trace of Giobbe from us — to human as well as architectural degradation. Having discovered the natural affinity between the stylistic qualities of etched images (particularly their comparative softness of line) and the physical textures of the ruins they represent, Piranesi was embarked — despite his intentions — on a career as an etcher as well as a designer, as a *vedutista* and *ruiniste* as well as a practicing architect, in the steps of Ricci and Vasi as well as Palladio.[40] Each image he produced, moreover, represents a double ruin: not through the traditional topos linking cultural and human decay (although that seems to be indisputably true of so many of these images), but rather in the sense that the process of physical deterioration we witness in his ruins is analogous to the etching process itself, which proceeds by immersing the varnished and inscribed copperplate in a bath of acid, which then bites into the copper surface the artist has exposed.

The role of acid in the printing process has often been associated with the corrosive, biting properties of visual satire, and Piranesi's own technique has been likened to the method of autopsy. He remains, in Hyatt Mayor's view, "the most dramatic dissector of ruins": he "went at Rome's weedy lumps of ruin like an anatomist at a cadaver, stripping, sectioning, sawing until he had established the structure in all its layers and functions."[41] In Barbara Stafford's more recent analogy, Piranesi "applied surgical procedures taken, I believe, from medical illustrations, to turn the still-living fabric of architecture inside out."[42] These metaphorical descriptions would work better, perhaps, if Piranesi had been an engraver, literally slicing, cutting, incising beneath the surface of his plate. Because he chose to work as an etcher, however, the process that enabled him to unearth the past was corrosive itself — not merely an antidote to loss, but a re-enactment of loss. Much of the softness we value in etchings, after all, is actually produced by the infiltration of acid beneath the varnish that has been applied to the copperplate.

Like the marble tablet of his revised title-page, Piranesi's copperplates were also vulnerable to the depredations of time. A plate that has been etched is much less durable than one that has been engraved, and the minor, "accidental" changes that Piranesi introduces into some of his prints may be aesthetically justified, but they also betray the fact that the copperplate — like the ruinous surfaces it represents — is itself prey to natural forces. The mechanical reproduction of the etched image, in which copy follows copy and issue follows issue, eventually works its own ruinous effects on a copperplate that must be reworked in order to offset the graphic loss through printing. Piranesi thought that he could print an extraordinary number of prints — as many as 4,000 — from each copperplate, a figure much higher than that of his contemporaries.[43] But the "astonishing resistance" of his plates (as Yourcenar puts it) must be carefully predicated on a style of etching that is relatively linear, forsaking the heavy crosshatching that tends to gather ink.[44] Piranesi would embrace the simplicity of this technique in his revision of the plates of the *Prima Parte* until the 1770s, when he would finally turn to a bolder, more accentuated style in which a sharp contrast between darks and lights replaced the subtle modulations of his earlier manner.[45]

Having begun its life as an "œuvre hétéroclite,"[46] the *Prima Parte* had, by the 1770s, long lost its own integrity as a codex. Having prefigured so many of Piranesi's later preoccupations — in subject, style, polemical edge, and even (as I have argued here) its self-conscious gesturing to its own graphic and cul-

tural instability — this slim volume was soon (and appropriately) absorbed into the growing corpus of his work, thereby
revealing his extraordinary habits of revision and cross-fertil-
ization. The *Prima Parte* ultimately figures not just the individual copperplate but the book itself as ruin, for the very success
of its images led Piranesi to incorporate it within other publications, beginning with the *Opera Varie* of 1750, just seven years
after its first appearance. Only a small handful of the original
copies of 1743 have survived, and most are incomplete. The rest
have themselves become fragments — *rovine d'antichi edifizi* —
ironic testimony to Piranesi's lifelong obsession with the fate of
cultural dissemination.

NOTES

1. John Wilton-Ely reminds me that Piranesi was the first to convey
the "layering of historical change" within a single image, normally by
inserting letters of the alphabet against relevant parts of a building's
structure; the letters, in turn, refer to extended captions within or outside of the print block. For an even broader discussion of what he calls
"vertical history," see the first chapter of Leonard Barkan's *Unearthing
the Past: Archaeology and Aesthetics in the Making of Renaissance Culture* (New Haven and London: Yale Univ. Press, 1999), in which he
argues that "Rome is almost purely a symbol. With the exception of a
very brief period, the history of Rome is a history of the idea of a city
that used to be" (p. 20).

2. Johann Wolfgang von Goethe, *Italian Journey,* trans. W. H. Auden
and Elizabeth Mayer (1962; rpt. Harmondsworth: Penguin Books,
1970), p. 133.

3. Edward Gibbon, *Memoirs of My Life,* ed. Georges A. Bonnard (London: Thomas Nelson, 1966), p. 136.

4. Marguerite Yourcenar, *"The Dark Brain of Piranesi" and Other Essays*, trans. Richard Howard (New York: Farrar, Straus, Giroux, 1984), p. 94.

5. Goethe, *Italian Journey*, trans. Robert R. Heitner, introd. Thomas P. Saine, eds. Thomas P. Saine and Jeffrey L. Sammons (New York: Suhrkamp Publishers, [1989]), p. 363: "This time our eyes greeted the pyramid of Cestius from outside, and the actual appearance of the ruined baths of Antoninus or Caracalla, of which Piranesi has given us so many a rich imaginary impression, could hardly satisfy even our artistically trained eye." (This passage is omitted in the Auden-Mayer translation, cited above). Goethe owned the first of the four volumes of the *Antichità Romane* (1756); see p. 475.

6. Horace Walpole, *Anecdotes of Painting*, 4th edn. (London, 1786), 4:398.

7. See Robison, *Piranesi: Early Architectural Fantasies, A Catalogue Raisonné of the Etchings* (Washington: National Gallery of Art; Chicago: Univ. of Chicago Press, 1986), p. 12, and Wilton-Ely, *The Mind and Art of Piranesi* (London: Thames and Hudson, 1978), pp. 12-13.

8. All quotations from Piranesi's dedicatory letter are drawn from *Giovanni Battista Piranesi: Drawings and Etchings at Columbia University*, exh. cat. (New York: Avery Architectural Library and Department of Art History and Archaeology, Columbia University, 1972), pp. 117-118. This text is not included in Piranesi, *Scritti di Storia e Teoria dell'Arte*, ed. Pierluigi Panza (Carnago: Sugarco Edizioni, 1993).

9. *Piranesi: Drawings and Etchings at Columbia University*, pp. 117-118. For a discussion of the contemporary architectural environment in Rome, see Manfredo Tafuri, *The Sphere and the Labyrinth: Avant-Gardes and Architecture from Piranesi to the 1970s*, trans. Pellegrino d'Acierno and Robert Connelly (Cambridge MA and London: MIT Press, 1987), p. 29 and passim.

10. See, for example, John Wilton-Ely, *The Mind and Art of Giovanni Battista Piranesi*, p. 12, and Nicholas Penny, *Piranesi* (1978; rpt. Lon-

don: Bloomsbury Books, 1988), p. 6. For an interesting discussion of Piranesi's relationship to the theatre, see Joseph R. Roach, Jr., "From Baroque to Romantic: Piranesi's Contribution to Stage Design," *Theatre Survey* 19 (1978): 91-118. Roach is particularly adept in pointing out the "chilling paradox" we find in the *carceri*: "these are prisons to which there are no precise boundaries, yet from which there is no escape" (p. 103).

11. Throughout this essay I follow Andrew Robison's invaluable and painstaking description of the various editions and issues of the *Prima Parte* in *Piranesi*; without Robison's extraordinarily detailed account of the progress of the plates, this essay could not have been written. Copies of the first issue of the *Prima Parte* are quite rare; my illustrations are drawn from the copy in the Houghton Library.

12. Robison, *Piranesi*, p. 17, points out that, in the *Rovine*, Piranesi "adds for the first time an inventive and distinctive technique: scratching the plate directly with a broad and coarse material (abrasive stone?) to produce multitudes of tiny lines and burr which print as a soft tone over the fountain bowl."

13. Robison, *Piranesi*, p. 67.

14. For the influence of Panini, see Wilton-Ely, *The Mind and Art of Piranesi*, p. 12. Piranesi would also share with Panini an interest in combining these imaginary buildings together as closely as possible (as in his intensely filled compositions such as the *Via Appia* in the *Antichità Romane*). Cf. Goethe's lament in the *Italian Journey*, trans. Auden and Mayer, p. 133: "Wherever you turn your eyes, every kind of vista, near and distant, confronts you — palaces, ruins, gardens, wildernesses, small houses, stables, triumphal arches, columns — all of them often so close together that they could be sketched on a single sheet of paper. One would need a thousand styluses to write with. What can one do here with a single pen?"

15. Armando Petrucci, *Public Lettering: Script, Power, and Culture*, trans. Linda Lappin (Chicago and London: Univ. of Chicago Press, 1993), p. 67, notes that the slanted dramatic perspective that we asso-

ciate with Piranesi's etched buildings — and, I would add, with the *scena per angolo* of contemporary set design — can also be seen in the slanted inscribed slabs of his title-pages.

16. I am grateful to John Wilton-Ely for this information about the Arcadi. For a recent study of the society, see Liliana Barroero and Stefano Susinno, "Arcadian Rome, Universal Capital of the Arts," in *Art in Rome in the Eighteenth Century*, ed. Edgar Peters Bowron and Joseph J. Rishel (London: Merrell Publishers; Philadelphia: Philadelphia Museum of Art, 2000), pp. 47-75. In the same catalogue, pp. 570-571, Malcolm Campbell briefly summarizes the affinity between Piranesi's etchings and the principles of the Arcadi.

17. Yourcenar, *"The Dark Brain of Piranesi" and Other Essays*, pp. 96-97.

18. For the most thorough discussion of Giobbe, see Georges Brunel, "Recherches sur les Débuts de Piranèse à Rome: Les Frères Pagliarini et Nicola Giobbe," in *Piranèse et Les Français*, ed. Brunel (Rome: Edizioni dell'Elefante for the French Academy in Rome, 1978), pp. 77-146.

19. *Piranesi: Drawings and Etchings at Columbia University*, p. 118.

20. See Wilton-Ely, *Piranesi as Architect and Designer* (New York: The Pierpont Morgan Library; New Haven and London: Yale Univ. Press, 1993), pp. 27-29. Petrucci, *Public Lettering*, p. 66 and figure 78, calls the obliteration of the dedication to Charlemont a form of *damnatio memoriae*.

21. Jonathan Scott, *Piranesi* (London: Academy Editions; New York: St. Martins Press, 1975), pp. 13 and 303, speculates that Giobbe may not have measured up to Piranesi's expectations of patronage.

22. Robison, *Piranesi*, p. 68, refers to them as "outline letters," markedly different from those in the first three states. Malcolm Campbell, who provides the helpful essay on "Piranesi and Innovation in Eighteenth-Century Roman Printmaking" in *Art in Rome in the Eighteenth Century*, ed. Bowron and Rishel (pp. 561-567), remarks in his catalogue essay for the title-page of the *Prima Parte* (p. 570) that the letters are "of a more Roman style." Campbell goes on to claim,

however, that the persistence of the "E" in "GIOBBE" "attests to the swiftness with which Piranesi must have reworked the plate" (p. 570), but microscopic analysis of the etching clearly shows that the letter "persisted" not because Piranesi was careless but precisely because he reworked it: it is qualitatively different from its predecessor in the previous state. Campbell also argues that the dedication to Giobbe disappeared because of the expansion of the original suite of plates into a combination volume, but such an explanation is not consistent with the publication history of the *Prima Parte*. The fourth state of the title page was first printed in 1748 (first edition, sixth issue), two years before it reappeared in the "combination volume" of the *Opera Varie* (see Robison, *Piranesi*, p. 68).

23. Petrucci, *Public Lettering*, p. 67.

24. See Penny, *Piranesi*, p. 9, who notes that in the later *vedute* "beggars appear to have overrun the city and prowl amid the debris waving dislocated arms in desperate conversation with deaf companions."

25. Wilton-Ely, *The Mind and Art of Piranesi*, p. 15, who points out that the only recorded paintings by Piranesi are studies of street figures, apparently executed in Naples.

26. Leon Battista Alberti, *On Painting*, trans. John R. Spencer (New Haven: Yale Univ. Press, 1956), p. 78.

27. Claude Gandelman, *Reading Pictures, Viewing Texts* (Bloomington and Indianapolis: Indiana Univ. Press, 1991), pp. 14-35.

28. I owe this point to Andrew Robison, in correspondence.

29. John Sparrow, *Visible Words: A Study of Inscriptions in and as Books and Works of Art* (Cambridge: Cambridge Univ. Press, 1969), pp. 85-88.

30. Petrucci, *Public Lettering*, p. 44.

31. Petrucci, *Public Lettering*, p. 44.

32. Louis Marin, "Towards a Theory of Reading in the Visual Arts: Poussin's *The Arcadian Shepherds*," in *Calligram: Essays in New Art*

History from France, ed. Norman Bryson (Cambridge: Cambridge Univ. Press, 1988), p. 81. Marin goes on to argue that the shepherd points exactly to the letter "r" in "Arcadia," an allusion to Cardinal Rospigliosi, who commissioned the painting and invented the phrase "Et in Arcadia ego" (p. 87). It is not impossible that Piranesi, with his interest in the arcane, might have known of such secretive gestures; it has even been suggested to me that the inverted letters in the text of his frontispiece refer to specific people.

33. W. J. T. Mitchell, *Picture Theory: Essays on Verbal and Visual Representation* (Chicago and London: Univ. of Chicago Press, 1994), pp. 76-77.

34. *Diderot Salons,* vol. 3, 1767, ed. Jean Seznec and Jean Adhémar (Oxford: Clarendon Press, 1963), pp. 228-229 (my translation). I owe this reference to Thomas McCormick, whose work on Clérisseau has also proven to be helpful. Cf. the new translation and edition by John Goodman: *Diderot on Art: Volume II, The Salon of 1767* (New Haven and London: Yale Univ. Press, 1995), pp. 198-199.

The scholarly literature on ruins is immense; for a useful bibliography, see Michael S. Roth with Claire Lyons and Charles Merewether, *Irresistible Decay: Ruins Reclaimed* (Los Angeles: Getty Research Institute, 1997), pp. 100-104. The focus of the various essays in their volume centers on the tension in ruins between presence and absence, transience and persistence; see, for example, pp. vii, xi, 25. Christopher Woodward, *In Ruins* (London: Chatto & Windus, 2001), p. 15, speculates that the fragmentary form of ruins forces spectators "to supply the missing pieces from his or her own imagination"; "a ruin therefore appears differently to everyone."

For the focus in literary studies on the fragmentary, incoherent, and incomplete nature of ruins, see, for instance, Thomas McFarland, *Romanticism and the Forms of Ruin: Wordsworth, Coleridge, and Modalities of Fragmentation* (Princeton: Princeton Univ. Press, 1981), David B. Morris, *Alexander Pope: The Genius of Sense* (Cambridge MA and London: Harvard Univ. Press, 1984), esp. p. 165 ("fragments are the natural setting of the philosophic mind"), and Anne Janowitz, *England's Ruins: Poetic Purpose and the National Landscape* (Oxford and Cambridge MA: Basil Blackwell, 1990).

35. Penny, *Piranesi*, p. 14.

36. Robert Etheridge Moore, "The Art of Piranesi: Looking Backward into the Future," in Robert E. Moore and Jean H. Hagstrum, *Changing Taste in Eighteenth-Century Art and Literature* (Los Angeles: William Andrews Clark Memorial Library, 1972), p. 20. See also Wilton-Ely, *The Mind and Art of Piranesi*, p. 41.

37. Yourcenar, *"The Dark Brain of Piranesi" and Other Essays*, p. 88.

38. Yourcenar, *"The Dark Brain of Piranesi" and Other Essays*, p. 100.

39. Yourcenar, *"The Dark Brain of Piranesi" and Other* Essays, p. 103; she must retreat from this argument by the foot of the same page, however, admitting that the figures "acquire, at least implicitly, a value as very minor symbols." For a general discussion of the relatively small role of didacticism in eighteenth-century landscape painting, see Kathleen Nicholson, *Turner's Classical Landscapes: Myth and Meaning* (Princeton: Princeton Univ. Press, 1990), pp. 7-12.

40. For the relationship of Piranesi's work to that of Ricci and Vasi, see: Wilton-Ely, *The Mind and Art of Piranesi*, p. 13; Wilton-Ely, *Piranesi as Architect and Designer*, p. 4; and Robison, *Piranesi*, p. 15.

41. A. Hyatt Mayor, *Giovanni Battista Piranesi* (New York: H. Bittner, 1952), p. 13.

42. Barbara Maria Stafford, *Body Criticism: Imaging the Unseen in Enlightenment Art and Medicine* (Cambridge MA: MIT Press, 1991), p. 59. Cf. Jennifer Bloomer's discussion of Piranesi's plan for his *magnifico collegio* in *Architecture and the Text: The (S)crypts of Joyce and Piranesi* (New Haven and London: Yale Univ. Press, 1993), p. 88: "Piranesi's plan . . . is a translucent slice, a window; also a slicer — Piranesi's critical knife, cutting open, laying bare, revealing."

43. See Mayor, *Giovanni Battista Piranesi*, p. 31. For an interesting discussion of early and late etching styles, the number of impressions taken from a plate, and the challenge of matching early and later prints for portfolio collections, see Peter Murray, *Piranesi and the Grandeur of Ancient Rome* (London: Thames & Hudson, 1971), pp. 39-43.

44. Yourcenar, *"The Dark Brain of Piranesi" and Other Essays*, p. 128.

45. See Robison, *Piranesi*, p. 24.

46. Jörg Garms, "Considérations sur la *Prima Parte*," in *Piranèse et Les Français*, ed. Brunel, p. 265.

Chapter 6
Antonioni's Blow-Up:
Implicated Artists and Unintentional Art

FIFTEEN YEARS have now passed since the release of
Antonioni's *Blow-Up*, and the controversies that first
engulfed the film show little sign of disappearing. But
whereas the film's original critics were often (and, I think, correctly) preoccupied with determining what *happened* in the
film (and in what order), more recent critics have tended to
argue that this is a moot point. Terry J. Peavler, for instance, has
recently contended that Antonioni is primarily interested in
questioning the nature of reality.[1] Like Cortázar (whose short
story he adapts), Antonioni combines two artistic forms, cin-

---

One of the highlights of my undergraduate education at Williams was the
opportunity to study film with Charles Thomas Samuels in an experimental
course entitled "Antonioni or Hitchcock?" Introducing the study of film to
advanced undergraduates in the humanities program at Northwestern was,
in turn, the most satisfying experience I have enjoyed as a teacher. This essay,
which had its origins in those long sessions in the dark in Williamstown in
January 1968, first appeared in the *Journal of Aesthetic Education* 16 (1982): 57-
67. Some of the more recent scholarship on *Blow-Up* has been intelligently
discussed and questioned by Lawrence Raab in his chapter in *Writers at the
Movies: Twenty-six Contemporary Authors Celebrate Twenty-six Memorable
Movies* (New York: HarperCollins, 2000), pp. 192-200.

ema and still photography, to explore a series of events that remains intractably ambiguous: "There is, in fact, so much evidence to prove or disprove the reality of almost anything that occurs in either work that the debate could rage endlessly without resolution," and Peavler singles out the murder in *Blow-Up* as "the single best example of ambiguity" in the film. Peavler believes that "it is difficult, if not impossible, to find two readers, or two viewers, who concur on what happens either in the story or in the film, much less come to agreement on what, if anything, it all means." But the problem with this kind of approach to *Blow-Up* is that, much as it focuses our attention on the film's epistemological questions, it simultaneously severs the connection between the process of knowing and the value of what is to be known. The narrative events in *Blow-Up* are surely not arbitrarily chosen; the terms in which Antonioni frames his drama here are no less moral than in his earlier films. As Antonioni has himself insisted, one of the major themes of the film is "to see or not to see properly the true *value* of things."[2]

In *Blow-Up*, Antonioni asks us to consider not only whether the camera remains a merely neutral observer or reflector of reality, but also whether it affects the humanity and accomplishment of the artist behind the lens. Intention and control are crucial in artistic terms as well as in the narrative sequence in which these aesthetic problems are posed: does the anonymous photographer have the ability (or the willingness) to act within the surprisingly violent world in which he suddenly finds himself? The photographer first believes he has prevented a murder from taking place; he later realizes his mistake, visits the body, attempts to pursue the murderer's accomplice, but becomes sidetracked in his quest; finally, admitting his failure, he disappears from the screen, a figure as inconsequential as the force of his actions. Antonioni's focus, however, is not simply on a man who refuses to protect a traditional social or moral order. The film suggests that the photographer is also implicated in the events his camera captures. He resembles both the actual murderer and, to the extent that he aspires to some artistic success, the other contemporary artists in the film. In large measure, his inability to comprehend what he has witnessed in the park is directly tied to his reliance on the technology of his art, a dilemma that the filmmaker — whose own medium of artistic expression is itself technological — must also face.

Antonioni's films open with ominous contrasts, often between the old and the new or between humans and a threatening background. *Blow-Up*, characteristically, opens with the jarring spectacle of a student "rag" group, vividly painted and dressed, miming its way through a once staid and formal London. Our introduction to the photographer-protagonist is no less unsettling or confusing. He is one of many overnight occupants of a London doss-house; only gradually does the camera isolate him from the rest of these drab and down-at-heels men, but his separation is startlingly complete when he tosses his newspapers (and camera) into the backseat of a Rolls Royce and drives away. We realize that he is a professional photographer, however, only when he arrives at his studio, which teems with suggestions of fashionable, frivolous life.

These two early images of the doss-house and the studio are connected, of course, by the photographer's vocation. The chic, remodeled studio represents the commercial world of fashion photography. The doss-house provides a setting for a different series of photographs of a more artistic (or at least more seri-

ous) nature, designed to form part of a book on the violence
and poverty of contemporary English life. The photographer
clearly has artistic ambitions, but his attitude toward the shots
he has taken of these aging men is uncomfortably close to his
glib and self-congratulatory patter about his fashion work:
"Why, they're fabulous! Go on. Yes. Yes. Great."[3] These photographs — which we later discover to be of sick and emaciated
men — are "studied" by the photographer as he finishes shav-
ing and praised as he presents his grimy clothing (another link
with the doss-house) to his assistant: "Here, you can burn that
lot." The photographs are brutal, dramatic, and effective; but we
sense that the men themselves have merely been exploited, their
old age, frailty, and poverty converted into "art" by the young.

We encounter this same tension between the possible uses of
the camera in the sequence that links the studio and the park.
The photographer is lured to the park by a commercial possi-
bility: he is interested in acquiring an antique store, protected by
an old man but soon to be sold by its young proprietor. The
photographer is excited by the store only as a business venture,
but his presence there sparks two rare moments of spontaneity
in the film. He decides he "must have" an enormous vintage
propeller he finds buried in a corner of the shop: "I can't live
without it." The propeller is a trendy technological prop whose
design, now that it is no longer functional, becomes a symbol of
the escape he craves. Eventually resting on the studio floor, the
propeller keeps company with large photographs of a skin-diver
and a parachutist; on the second floor, a photograph of a camel
caravan stretches along one of the walls. Like the fashion model
(Verushka) and the girl who owns the antique store, the photographer has "gone off" London; he desires escape into a new
world, even if he admits to the girl that other places, like Nepal,
are "all antiques."

Even more seductive than the propeller, however, is the lush park that faces the store. Camera in hand, the photographer begins to explore this quieter world. He first passes a groundskeeper, a woman dressed like (and curiously resembling) a man. He will eventually discover that other appearances in the park are also misleading. As he stalks a group of birds, "shooting" them with his camera, he shifts his attention to a pair of lovers, headed for another region of the park. The photographer discovers the couple conducting their dalliance amid an incredibly green and luxuriant world. Sensing the beauty of the scene, he crouches behind a wooden fence and photographs the young woman and her much older lover. He later creeps closer to his quarry, stalking them tree by tree. Finally, as he attempts to withdraw from the drama enacted before him, he is followed by the young woman, now obviously distraught. She demands the roll of film he has taken, but he refuses to give it up. She is persistent, but suddenly flees when she notices that her lover has disappeared. The photographer watches her run to the spot where the couple had previously embraced. There, at her feet, is the body of her older lover. But the photographer notices only the woman, now running out of the picture. His camera, however, has recorded the entire scene.

The photographer is intrigued by what he has witnessed, but his attention is soon diverted by the giant propeller in the antique shop. Only when he joins his agent for lunch does he return to the drama he has seen. He tells Ron that these photographs of a peaceful and lyrical moment will represent a "truer" conclusion to his otherwise depressing and violent book. But just as he tyrannically orders lunch (he seems never to finish a drink or meal), he notices a young man who peers into the restaurant at him and then inspects his car. From the back, at least, this young blond man closely resembles the photographer; he is, we later surmise, the young woman's accomplice, the actual murderer in the park. Roused again by interest, the photographer carefully leads the woman back to his studio. Hoping to unravel the mystery, he parks his car in the alley as the camera draws our attention to the conspicuously painted "39" of his address (an apparent allusion to Hitchcock's mystery *The Thirty-Nine Steps*). But his encounter with the woman solves no puzzles; it only whets his appetite. After considerable parrying, they apparently make love.[4] As she leaves, they exchange false confidences: she gives him an incorrect telephone number; he gives her the wrong roll of film.

The photographer's curiosity has been aroused. After developing the roll of film, he becomes intrigued by the direction of the young woman's gaze as she embraces her older lover (this is one point at which Antonioni carefully follows the text of his otherwise changed source, "The Devil's Spittle") and discovers that her eyes point directly to something hidden in the bushes behind the wooden fence. Reproducing each section of the film and eventually enlarging each frame, he finally sees the source of her anxiety: concealed by the foliage behind the park fence stands a man pointing a revolver at the young woman's lover. The photographer finally breaks the spell of tension and excitement that Antonioni has carefully woven in this scene. The walls of the studio, filled with the glossy enlargements, have provided a natural stage for this drama. Antonioni's camera, panning back and forth from photographer to photograph, has become a skillful narrator, providing a temporal framework for the frozen characters of the blow-ups. The photographer's response to his discovery is euphoric. He calls his friend and agent, Ron, to share his excitement: "Something fantastic's happened. Those photographs in the park . . . fantastic. . . . Somebody was trying to kill somebody else. I saved his life . . . ." But the photographer's conclusion is premature. The dead man's body can be seen among the enlarged photographs; the photographer has only begun to comprehend fully the drama he has witnessed or to analyze the photographs he has taken.

Our discovery of why the photographer has failed to "see" correctly is crucial to our understanding of the film. His misprision begins in the park. Because he does not order or design the scene he films, he is at first able to see only so far into the drama enacted before him. Design, order, control, intention — all the elements we normally assume the artist to possess — belong more properly here to the murderers. The photographer has only accidentally stumbled upon the scene; he simply documents it with his camera, accepting it at face value. And this in turn poses critical (and often pedagogical) problems for us as viewers of the film. Because we also have difficulty spotting the dead man's body on the ground — even when we freeze the film in a frame-by-frame analysis — we may claim that Antonioni places unrealistic demands upon both the photographer's and our own abilities. In believing this, however, we miss Antonioni's point: the photographer has become, like us, a merely passive viewer of the scene before him. Even the design and control he exercises in his fashion photography now elude him; he sees only so much and counts on his camera alone to preserve it.

But the camera, of course, sees and records much more. In this case, at least, the photographs have preserved the entire drama. They are neutral documents, however; the photographer must interpret them himself. And this, it seems, accounts for his second failure in perception. Examining the series of blow-ups, he is slowly able to piece together the puzzle. The photographs have preserved what he, as viewer, had missed. In calling his friend Ron, he in effect congratulates himself. In "solving" the puzzle, he believes that he had earlier (and unwittingly) prevented a murder.

But the photographer, of course, has uncovered only part of the drama's entire design. His discovery of the body in the photographs — and with it the discovery that his own knowledge has been acquired too late — comes to him only after his sexual trysts with the two aspiring models. Antonioni's ordering of events is revealing: he seems to argue that impediments to full understanding still remain. The two girls literally interrupt the photographer's progress; sizing them up, he almost forgets that he has been sharing his discovery with Ron on the telephone (and Ron, of course, has long since hung up). We realize how easily the photographer is sidetracked. But the girls' arrival is not a simple interruption: their sexual diversion suggests moral implications. The photographer suddenly sits up and sees the body in the blow-up only *after* he has finished with the girls. He is framed by a girl on each side and, in the foreground, by two of the enlarged photographs. As Charles Thomas Samuels first pointed out, Antonioni emphasizes the connection between this sexual diversion and postponed discovery by his careful use of color: the two darkrooms the photographer uses to develop his film have green and purple doors; the two girls wear green and purple tights.[5]

The photographer now appears before us in a diminished capacity. His own limitations and the temptations surrounding him have prevented him from understanding the deadly intentions behind a seemingly innocent and pastoral drama. His inspection of the dead man's body proves his camera to have been correct, but the rest of the film documents the moral impotence of his sidetracked quest. Accidentally spotting the female murderer in a ticket line, the photographer parks his car and enters a rock club, yet another dead end in his pursuit.

Here, however, he is caught up in the crowd's excitement as the Yardbirds begin to destroy their musical instruments. Ever competitive, the photographer emerges from the club with a fitting symbol of his quest: the broken neck of an electric guitar, another useless artifact (like the propeller), this one to be quickly discarded. The subsequent scenes at the pot party reinforce his frustration and ultimate complicity. Unable to persuade Ron to help him, the photographer also succumbs to the temptations of drug-induced escape. Rising alone in the stately house the next morning, he views a scene of devastation seemingly modeled on the "morning after" plates of Hogarth's "progresses." Finding that the body has been removed from the park, he once again visits the area near the tennis courts where he had earlier photographed the birds. As the actors mime a game of tennis, the photographer first appears aloof, then pleasantly cooperative as he throws an imaginary tennis ball back into the court. Finally, and unmistakably, his eyes betray a more serious interest in the game, and the soft "pucks" of tennis balls on the soundtrack suggest that he has joined the charade in earnest. Appropriately, the camera distances us from him by raising us above the green swath of the park. The photographer is isolated, like the dead man's body, against a ground of green; and, like the dead man, he suddenly disappears.

The photographer's final visit to the scene of the crime and the suggestive closing shots of the film clearly emphasize Antonioni's insistence that the protagonist is implicated in the events he records. Antonioni suggests at several points that the photographer shares a moral complicity in the drama his camera observes. His photographs of London's derelicts both capture their plight and explain it. These older men remind us of the central drama of the film in which an older lover is destroyed by the young. The photographer, who is both young himself and shares the sexual mores of the young, makes love — or at least intends to make love — to the murderer's accomplice. Significantly, as he compliments her on her posture and composure, he models her against a purple backdrop in his studio. Later he will make love to the two younger girls on this very "set." Purple becomes the ground on which sex and sexuality are framed; similarly, green becomes the ground on which murder is framed. The opening credits portray a sinuous, writhing dancer viewed through the holes of a grass-green screen. The photographer shoots the birds against a green plot of grass. The body of the murdered man disappears from a similar plot. The final shot is of the photographer, framed against a similar background from which he finally, and mercifully, disappears.[6]

The narrative thus suggests that the photographer unconsciously places himself in the role of the murderer. He resembles him in appearance, as a lover, and as a stalker in the park. (Antonioni even stresses their similarity by having each quickly swoop by the window of the restaurant.) At the root of their similarity is their mutual reliance on a mechanical object — revolver or camera — pointed through a wooden fence at an unsuspecting quarry. Both "shoot" their subject; both are overshadowed by a mysterious neon sign that vaguely suggests a giant gun. Even the language of photography suggests the shared violence of this association: the enlargements that make the photographer's discovery possible are innocently called "blow-ups."

Antonioni thus finally suggests the broader implication of the artist who loses the ordering force of his art and, with it, the ability to exert a moral force as well. The artist finds himself at the mercy of his artistic medium. Although reality is neutrally presented to the artist by his camera, the camera no longer merely serves him as an artistic tool. In a sense, Antonioni's photographer serves the camera; the artist's limitations place him in a subservient position where he must wrestle to achieve an understanding of the properties of his own art. Uncontrolled by the artist's ordering intelligence, observed reality on the other side of the camera will conform to other designs and intentions. The artist becomes a mere interpreter, unable to exert his own influence on the scene his camera captures.

The photographer, however, is not alone in his dilemma; *Blow-Up* provides two striking parallels in contemporary painting and music. The photographer's friend Bill, who lives across the alley, is a derivative painter whose canvases suggest a dripping or splattering technique similar to pointillism. Analyzing his works, Bill reveals an ignorance of their initial conception and development that is precariously close to the photographer's: "They don't mean anything when I do them — just a mess. Afterwards I find something to hang on to ... like ... like that leg. And then it sorts itself out. It adds up. It's like finding a clue in a detective story." Like the painter, the photographer must also sort things out. In his case, the arm of the murderer and the body of the murdered man finally put his canvas in order. And, as the painter's wife points out, her husband's work resembles the dotted configurations — the screen — of the photographer's enlargements. The painter and photographer, moreover, share their limitations with musicians. The Yardbirds also find themselves at the mercy of their electronic equipment. When it fails them, one musician destroys his guitar in frustration (and as a conscious performance). Significantly, the violence of his action finally generates excitement among the audience. Music, like painting, punctuates the film. The songs of the soundtrack actually summarize the action (and inaction) of the narrative: the models are photographed to the sounds of "Did you ever have to make up your mind?"; the receptionist's radio wails "Didn't know you had troubles / Got my feet in the water"; the Yardbirds sing "Stroll On."

The focus of the film, however, is appropriately on photography. In large measure, Antonioni's film is an exploration of the possibilities and dangers of the photographic image. The photographer wields a peculiarly modern means of expression, and Antonioni's analysis of its strengths and limitations mirrors Siegfried Kracauer's discussion of photography in his *Theory of Film: The Redemption of Physical Reality*. Summarizing early beliefs about photography, Kracauer claims that this new artistic form holds three distinct appeals for us: it produces documents of unquestionable authenticity; it produces discoveries unavailable even to the photographer himself; and it provides a source of beauty. Kracauer's discussion of this second point nicely captures the drama of Antonioni's film: "Think of the satisfaction people are deriving from the scrutiny of an enlargement in which, one by one, things emerge they would not have suspected in the original print — nor in reality itself, for that matter. This too is a typical reaction to photographs. In fact, we tend to look at them in the hope of detecting something new and unexpected — a confidence which pays tribute to the camera's revealing faculty." And continual discovery, Kracauer argues, visits both the viewer of the photograph and its maker.[7]

Kracauer's analysis of the photographic image provides an interesting perspective on *Blow-Up*, even if the book's general arguments have not held up as well. Parker Tyler has intelligently questioned Kracauer's work, but Tyler's analysis of *Blow-Up* in this context seems not to penetrate far enough: "We perceive, if we detect the true meaning of Antonioni's device, how vain would be Kracauer's protest that *Blow-Up* vindicates his conception of the photograph as self-sufficient chronicler of reality."[8] Tyler points out that Antonioni's photographer is really a second-rate maker of fantasies and high camp, but in a sense he misses the point. This photographer is neither a redeemer of physical reality nor a successful artist. On the one hand, his camera actually does record what he fails to see; attempting to understand his photographs, he continues to encounter limitations in his "vision." The photograph does lead him to a real body; it does bring him to a heightened sense of his own deficiencies; but it does not, finally, change the nature of a man unequipped to act (or create) in a decisive way. On the other hand, the photographic image is more than a mere recording of the physical world. But the protagonist is a fashion photographer, fashionably disaffected, pursuing a career designed to celebrate that which is ephemeral (like the architect Sandro in *L'Avventura,* he bases his work upon a principle of planned obsolescence). He appears to be good at what he does, but even the quasi-sexual encounter with Verushka suggests his chic but cheap counterfeiting of "reality." His intended volume of serious photographs is both callous and imitative. It reveals an eye for brutality that we have no reason to believe the photographer himself possesses. His own world is too easy; the photographs are merely "super." Their casual brutality reflects his own contemptuous language and behavior. Even in the choice of a final image for his volume he misunderstands the nature of his work: because he fails to acknowledge its brutality, the image of a seemingly idyllic moment becomes the most ironic and damning fact in his book.

If this argument has occasionally seemed too stark a simplification of the film's rich texture, we must remember that Antonioni often forces us to think in general, almost abstract terms.

Beneath the lively surface of the film we are asked to view the almost allegorical nature of the characters and their actions. The very namelessness of the characters demands that we awkwardly refer to them as "the photographer," "the murderer," "the victim." And, perhaps to the embarrassment of our critical discourse, even the events must be carefully summarized and unfolded. But even this attempt to elucidate the general argument of the film has its limitations. Antonioni never explicitly links the photographer and the murderer: he relies on the implications of his narrative and images to make his point.

Throughout the film Antonioni carefully weaves a web of intentions in which moral and artistic control are implicitly linked; his characters intend to do one thing but almost always end up doing something else. The photographer's search for the girl, the murderer's accomplice, is subverted much like Sandro's quest for Anna in *L'Avventura*. The photographer intends to follow the girl by entering a rock concert, but he is soon caught up in the violence and hysteria of the crowd. He intends to ask his friend Ron for assistance, but instead succumbs to the temptations of the party. Verushka intends to fly to Paris, but instead finds her Paris through drugs. The photographer does not intend to have sex with the girl when she offers it in exchange for his roll of film; later, when he does harbor sexual intentions, the action is interrupted by the arrival of the propeller. The photographer exercises full control over himself and his "art" only when he photographs the models in his studio. There he carefully orders their poses and background and then intentionally leaves them with their eyes tightly closed. His strict control over this narrow world is neatly captured in his first encounter with the two aspiring models: his trick with the coin mirrors his control over himself and the girls' expectations. But in the more serious and deadly aspects of the action — photography in the park and prevention or solution of murder — his intentions are never fulfilled. His moral imperative to do something is, like Sandro's, easily blunted; escape lies too comfortably at hand.

Ironically, the achievement of *Blow-Up* lies in Antonioni's ability to create a film that ultimately refutes the very dangers and limitations it exposes. Whereas Antonioni's protagonist is unable to order the elements of his art, Antonioni himself exercises the strictest control over his camera, screenplay, soundtrack, actors, and technicians.[9] Although *L'Avventura* is often said to explore a new language for the cinema, Antonioni has been rather conservative in his experiments with cinematic technique. His first use of the flashback occurs, surprisingly, only in his latest film, *The Passenger*; he waited until *Deserto Rosso* to introduce color. But in each case the result has been well worth our wait and the filmmaker's painstaking care. The flashback sequence in *The Passenger* is one of the most brilliant in film; characteristically, Antonioni's use of color in *Deserto Rosso* became, in its own way, part of the film's actual subject.

Antonioni's control over the backgrounds of *Blow-Up* has been justly celebrated: the entire park was painted a luxuriant green for the specific effect he desired (this in contrast, of course, to the photographer's casual use of the grassy plot as a background for his own "work"). Entire neighborhoods appear to have been painted, as well as the cars and buses that run through them. The photographer's studio is a study in skillful composition. Even the brown wooden supports against which the characters lean suggest the enigmatic neon sign ("FOA") that Antonioni erected above the park. Much of the film's importance derives from the ambition and richness of its own subject. But, as the film's own themes suggest, such ambition and richness are wasted if they cannot be tightly ordered and fashioned by the artist's controlling intelligence. Within this larger irony lies yet another: in the celebrated "orgy" scene, just as our attention is riveted on the photographer's exploits with the two girls, we can see one of Antonioni's workmen in the upper right-hand corner of the screen. Antonioni has acknowledged the workman's accidental entry into the film, and yet the filmmaker remains amused rather than disturbed. In a sense, this one flaw functions both as an ultimate irony in the film and, because it is an exception, as a reminder of the stringent artistic control that marks Antonioni's ultimate success.

NOTES

1. Terry J. Peavler, "*Blow-Up*: A Reconsideration of Antonioni's Infidelity to Cortázar," *PMLA* 94 (1979): 887-893 (I quote from p. 888). Peavler, like John Freccero (see note 9), is best when discussing the self-conscious nature of Antonioni's film; he sees *Blow-Up* as the equivalent of Fellini's *8 ½* or Bergman's *Persona*. Much of the best criticism on the film has been collected by Roy Huss, *Focus on "Blow-Up"* (Englewood Cliffs NJ: Prentice-Hall, 1971), including Charles Thomas Samuels's "*The Blow-Up*: Sorting Things Out," to which I am indebted at many points. I have also profited from Marsha Kinder's sensitive discussion of *Blow-Up* in the context of Antonioni's career; see "Antonioni in Transit," *Sight and Sound* 36 (Summer 1967): 132-137, reprinted in Huss, *Focus on "Blow-Up,"* pp. 78-88.

2. Quoted from "Antonioni — English Style," in "*Blow-Up*": *A Film by Michelangelo Antonioni*, Modern Film Scripts (London: Lorrimer, 1971), p. 14, my emphasis.

3. All quotations are from the filmscript.

4. This appears to be the one fully ambiguous moment in the film, even if the intentions of the two characters are finally clear. Peavler

asks if the photographer makes love with *anyone* (the accomplice, his neighbor Patricia, or the teenage girls). There is clearly no indication that he makes love with Patricia, much as she might wish him to; his dalliance with the girls, on the other hand, appears fairly certain, especially when we remember the codified restraints within which Antonioni was working in 1966.

5. Charles Thomas Samuels, "*The Blow-Up*: Sorting Things Out," in *Focus on "Blow-Up,"* p. 23.

6. Henry Fernández, "*Blow-Up*: From Cortázar to Antonioni: Study of an Adaptation," *Film Heritage* 4, no. 2 (1968-69): 30, argues that as the film and story close, "both men have learned the limitations of their media and will now move in a world beyond the grasp of their cameras." But this is surely not consistent with Antonioni's insistent diminution of his character at the end of *Blow-Up.*

7. Siegfried Kracauer, *Theory of Film: The Redemption of Physical Reality* (London: Oxford Univ. Press, 1960), p. 21.

8. Parker Tyler, "Masterpieces by Antonioni and Bergman," in *Film Theory and Criticism*, ed. Gerald Mast and Marshall Cohen (New York: Oxford Univ. Press, 1971), p. 55.

9. John Freccero begins to approach this interpretation in his suggestive essay: "Thomas [the photographer] is perhaps the portrait of the director as a young director and his failure is Antonioni's subsequent triumph." See *"Blow-Up*: From the Word to the Image," *Yale/Theatre* 3 (Fall 1970): 15-24 (I quote from p. 19). The photographic image differs, of course, from the cinematic image (or sequence of images), and Antonioni appears to acknowledge this difference when his photographer attempts to make sense of the blow-ups in his studio. In many ways, this is the most intriguing and daring scene in the film; even the accompanying sounds of jazz fade out as the photographer is forced to exercise his vision for the first time. The scene is stark, silent, and intellectual. The individual photograph, however, cannot reveal the entire drama. The photographer relies on the narrative formed by succeeding photographs and blow-ups; we, in the audience, rely on Antonioni's cutting between photograph and photographer. On a

small scale, photography "becomes" cinema as the protagonist struggles to put these separate images together, to re-create a narrative he
only partially understood in the first place.

Part Three

Chapter 7

The Making of Johnson's
"Life of Collins"

ECAUSE he was himself a poet and counted many
literary figures among his friends, William Collins could
have been expected to be remembered in print by several of the major writers of the mid-eighteenth century. But
Joseph Warton, who knew Collins longest and perhaps best, left
no account of his friend's life even though their work was
closely related at several important moments in their careers.[1]
The sketches of Collins by Thomas Warton, John Ragsdale, and
Gilbert White were all written much later in the century, long
after Collins's death in 1759. The account of Collins upon which

---

This chapter and the three that follow all have their origins, either directly or
indirectly, in my dissertation at Princeton, which was a critical edition of the
poetry of William Collins. The late Louis Landa kindly told me that a graduate student should choose a dissertation subject with whom he could live
for the rest of his or her scholarly career — and he certainly didn't have
Collins in mind. Ironically, however, the issues involved in editing Collins's
poetry (especially the problem of capitalization and italics, which is
addressed in the next three essays) have remained of considerable interest to
me, often pointing me in new directions. The current essay was first published in *The Papers of the Bibliographical Society of America* 74 (1980): 95-115.

scholars have relied most heavily — for its biographical information, for its careful judgment of Collins's character, and for
its strictures on his poetry — has been Samuel Johnson's, first
printed in 1763 and then expanded in the more substantial (and
more objective) life of 1781. Johnson's "Life of Collins" has long
served as one of the most useful sources for readers interested in
Collins and his poetry, but surprisingly little analysis has been
devoted to this biographical sketch by those whose primary
interest is Johnson. An examination of the making of the "Life
of Collins" raises issues that are of some importance in our estimate of Johnson as a biographer, as a proofreader, and as a
reviser of his own work. At several points the "Life of Collins"
poses, at least in miniature, many of the textual dilemmas to be
found throughout the *Lives of the English Poets*. A collation of
the various versions of the life suggests, moreover, that in revising his early sketch of Collins for the later portrait, Johnson
worked from a corrupt text that restricted his access to important biographical information.

I

Johnson's preliminary "Character" of Collins appeared in the
twelfth (and final) volume of the *Poetical Calendar* (December
1763), a publication that was meant to serve as a supplement to
Robert Dodsley's highly successful *Collection of Poems by Several Hands* (1748-58).[2] The *Poetical Calendar* was the work of
Francis Fawkes and William Woty, who issued one volume each
month during 1763 and then attempted to duplicate their feat
the following year with the *Poetical Magazine, or the Muses'
Monthly Companion* (it ran only through June). Fawkes's and
Woty's miscellany included several of Collins's poems that had
been omitted by Dodsley; John Langhorne, who reviewed it

enthusiastically in the *Monthly Review* in 1765, was apparently stimulated by it to issue the first "complete" edition of Collins's poetry the following year, published with a substantial critical commentary. Fawkes (1720-77) was a clergyman and poet who had gained some fame as the translator of Anacreon, Sappho, Bion, Moschus, and Musaeus in 1760. Johnson is reported to have said that Fawkes translated Anacreon "very finely";[3] in the preface to his translation of the *Idylliums* of Theocritus (1767), Fawkes in turn credited Johnson with having corrected part of his work and praised him for including some "judicious remarks."[4] Woty (1731?-91), on the other hand, was a Grub Street versifier whose connections with writers like Johnson are much less clear and were presumably (by 1763) much less intimate.

Many of Collins's poems were collected in the eleventh volume of this miscellany (in November), and at some point — perhaps even as an afterthought — a brief memoir of the poet was presumably requested as an accompaniment to the remaining verses to be published the following month. "Some Account of the Life and Writings of Mr. William Collins" is the work of two hands: the second half of this six-page biography was written by Johnson, who is introduced (anonymously) as "a gentleman, deservedly eminent in the republic of letters, who knew him [Collins] intimately well"; the first half of the account, which is largely biographical, was written by James Hampton. Hampton (1721-78) had entered Winchester College only a year before Collins (in 1733), and they were also contemporaries at Oxford (Collins was at Queen's and then Magdalen, Hampton was at Corpus Christi, and their friends Gilbert White and Joseph Warton were at Oriel). White, who has provided our only firsthand report of Collins's life at the university, characterized Hampton as "a member of a certain college, as remarkable at that time for his brutal disposition as for his good scholarship," and his account of Hampton's behavior at a "tea-visit" in Collins's rooms clearly justifies his opinion.[5] But Hampton's "good scholarship" eventually reached fruition, and his translation of Polybius was quite favorably reviewed by Johnson in the *Literary Magazine* in 1756.[6]

Both halves of the memoir of Collins were mistakenly thought to be the work of Joseph Warton. When Johnson's "Character" was reprinted in *Miscellanous and Fugitive Pieces* in 1773, a reviewer in the *Gentleman's Magazine* wrote that it was "first printed in the Poetical Calendar for December, 1763, and, we think, communicated to Mr. Fawkes (the editor) by Dr. Joseph Warton."[7] But a subsequent letter to the *Gentleman's* from "Academicus" of Oxford (Thomas Warton) pointed out both that the "Character" of Collins had been written by John-son and that it had been reprinted in that very magazine in 1764.[8] Similarly, when Thomas Percy supplied Boswell with a list of "The Publications Fugitive Pieces etc. of Mr. Samuel Johnson" in 1772, he accurately attributed the correct pages of the "Account" to Johnson but specified, "The former part [was] by Jo. Warton."[9] Apparently dissatisfied with Percy's report, Boswell later wrote to Joseph Warton himself: "I think Sir you men[tione]d to me that you might perhaps find among your pap[er]s something concern[ing] Collins. If you do I beg you may favour me with it. Pray was the orig[inal] *Life of Collins* all written by Johnson or did you furnish a part of it as I have been told?"[10] We do not have Warton's reply to Boswell's letter, but Boswell was careful to distinguish Johnson's share in the mem-oir when he listed it among Johnson's publications in his *Life*.[11] It is probable that many of Collins's friends — including John-son himself — knew that Hampton was the author of the biog-raphical portion of the sketch. Hampton's authorship was known to John Mulso, who delivered his opinion to Gilbert

White in a letter of 2 April 1764: "I have read Collins's Life. Not enough is said, if it was right to say any Thing at all: His Genius is not enough called forth to Light, to whet ye Reader to buy one of his Works. As to Hampton, we had always a Dislike to ye Man, tho' ingenious, & his present Life does not take off that Prevention."[12]

Much of Hampton's "Account" does bear out Mulso's opinion, but Hampton, to his credit, had clearly engaged in some research concerning Collins's life. He documents the poet's birth at Chichester, his family's circumstances, his education at Winchester and Oxford; he provides a portrait of Collins in London that is not unlike Johnson's more famous description of the young "literary adventurer"; he introduces Collins's first published poem, and he is the first to mention Collins's plans for a tragedy, for *The History of the Revival of Learning*, and for a translation of Aristotle's *Poetics*. But at least one piece of information — the incorrect report of Collins's death in 1756 — suggests that Hampton had long been out of touch with Collins; and other comments, interspersed throughout the biographical sketch, suggest that Hampton had very little sympathy for Collins or his work. Hampton praises the short piece addressed "To Miss Aurelia C — r" as a poem displaying "a genius, and turn of expression, very rarely to be met with in juvenile compositions," but his normal tone is one of waspish disapproval of Collins's literary ambitions:

About the year 1743, he left Oxford, having taken the degree of bachelor of arts, weary of the confinement and uniformity of an academical life; fondly imagining that a man of parts was sure of making his fortune in London; and struck with the name of author and poet, without consulting his friends, he immediately removed to town, and rashly resolved to live by his pen, without undertaking the drudgery of any profession.

Hampton's closing words again reveal a barely restrained hostility that colors his entire remembrance of his friend: "For a man of such an elevated genius, Mr. Collins has wrote but little: his time was chiefly taken up in laying extensive projects, and vast designs, which he never even begun to put in execution."

Hampton's tone may indeed sound spiteful, but there is more than an element of truth in his depiction of Collins's procrastination and his fondness for devising grand designs that seldom found their way into print. It is not surprising, therefore, that Johnson, even as he attempted to soften Hampton's account of Collins in the following "Character" of his friend, was nevertheless forced to focus on many of the limitations that Hampton had already introduced. Johnson opens with an examination of Collins's poetical character. Collins was a man "of extensive literature, and of vigorous faculties," well read in several languages, but he "had employed his mind chiefly upon works of fiction, and subjects of fancy; and, by indulging some peculiar habits of thought, was eminently delighted with those flights of imagination which pass the bounds of nature . . . ." Johnson's strictures on Collins's poetry — and his general antipathy to this new school of English verse — are well known, but it is worth noting (especially in light of Hampton's hostility) how often Johnson's commentary is essentially protective in nature. Diligence is never wholly lost, Johnson argues: "if his efforts sometimes caused harshness and obscurity, they likewise produced in happier moments sublimity and splendour." Collins's poems often deviate "in quest of mistaken beauties," but they are nonetheless the "productions of a mind not deficient in fire, nor unfurnished with knowledge either of books or life . . . ."

Much the same tone of reconciliation informs the remaining pages of Johnson's sketch. Turning to Collins's character, Johnson observes that his morals were pure and his opinions pious; but, "In a long continuance of poverty, and long habits of dissipation, it cannot be expected that any character should be exactly uniform." But Johnson proceeds to characterize Collins's weaknesses — such as they were — as the consequence of "unexpected pressure, or casual temptation"; his principles remained unshaken. Similarly, he qualifies Hampton's account of Collins's "nervous disorder . . . with which . . . his head and intellects were at times affected" by pointing out that "The latter part of his life cannot be remembered but with pity and sadness." Johnson observes that Collins "languished some years under that depression of mind which enchains the faculties without destroying them, and leaves reason the knowledge of right, without the power of pursuing it," a description much more sympathetic — and much more frightening — than that offered by Hampton.[13] And Johnson closes his narrative by recording his meeting with Collins at Islington, where his friend, awaiting the arrival of his sister, showed Johnson the Bible he had been reading: "'I have but one book,' says Collins, 'but that is the best.'" It is a touching anecdote, one that concludes Johnson's memoir by emphasizing Collins's lucidity and piety.

It is uncertain whether it was Hampton or Fawkes who requested this character sketch from Johnson, but it is clear that one (or both) of them believed that Hampton's account should be supplemented by someone who knew Collins better during his productive years. In all truth, however, Johnson had fallen out of touch with Collins in the 1750s, even though he wrote to him (without a reply) and continually inquired about him in letters to the Wartons.[14] But Johnson seems to have had little time to make inquiries when he wrote his short piece for the *Poetical Calendar,* and one incorrect statement — concerning Collins's retirement to the care of his sister in Colchester — was included in the memoir.

The expansion of this character sketch in the *Prefaces, Biographical and Critical, to the Works of the English Poets* in 1781 enabled Johnson to furnish a fuller and more accurate history of his friend, and in the opening paragraph of this enlarged sketch he stressed his indebtedness for various information to Joseph Warton. Like many of Johnson's biographical studies, the "Life of Collins" is divided into three parts: the first section, roughly the length of the original "Character," is primarily biographical; the "Character" is then reprinted with only minor changes; and the final section, shorter than the first two, represents a reconsideration of Collins's illness and his poetry (his first published poem is included at the very end).

The biographical section appears to be closely modeled on Hampton's account; it is primarily a chronological study that repeats much of Hampton's information while providing additional details at several points. The opening paragraphs of Hampton's and Johnson's lives are in fact uncannily similar, and it is natural to conclude that here, as elsewhere, Johnson made what use he could of previous accounts in writing his own *Lives of the English Poets.* Hampton wrote: "Mr. William Collins was born at Chichester in Sussex, in the year 1721: in which city his father was a reputable tradesman. He was admitted a scholar of Winchester college, Feb. 23, 1733. where he spent seven years under the care of the learned Dr. Burton." Johnson specifies the kind of tradesman Collins's father was, supplies the poet's birthday (but not the correct year), and generally seems to recast much of Hampton's prose: "William Collins was born at Chichester on the twenty-fifth of December, about 1720. His father was a hatter of good reputation. He was in 1733, as Dr. Warton has kindly informed me, admitted scholar of Winchester College, where he was educated by Dr. Burton."[15] Hampton had claimed that Collins's "Latin exercises were never so much admired as his English"; Johnson remarks, "His English exercises were better than his Latin."

Johnson's own voice becomes more distinctly audible in the short comments he often inserts between the biographical passages. Noting that there was no vacancy at New College for Collins in 1740, Johnson states, "This was the original misfortune of his life." Observing that Collins designed many works but seemed to pursue no settled purpose, he characteristically remarks, "A man, doubtful of his dinner, or trembling at a creditor, is not much disposed to abstracted meditation, or remote enquiries." In general, Johnson's life of Collins picks up in interest — and in confidence of appraisal — when the biographer turns to those years when he knew his subject well, and when they shared many of their disappointments and much of their impoverishment together. It is Johnson's personal touch, in fact, that helps bring Collins to life in ways that Hampton's account was unable to do. Like Hampton, Johnson describes Collins's plans for a translation of the *Poetics,* but he is able to add, at the same time, a humorous description of the circumstances that necessitated Collins's work as a classical translator and commentator. Johnson also mentions Collins's published proposals for *The History of the Revival of Learning* and, like Hampton, he too admits that "probably not a page of the History was ever written," but his recollection that he had heard Collins "speak with great kindness of Leo the Tenth, and with keen resentment of his tasteless successor" invests Collins with a greater sincerity in his various literary projects. What Johnson characteristically brings to his "Life of Collins" is not only a fund of personal knowledge and pleasant remembrance, but a sense, as well, of a larger perspective in which Collins's work and personal calamities should be viewed. There is a sympathetic irony here that is Johnson's alone: "But man is not born for happiness. Collins, who, while he *studied to live,* felt no evil but poverty, no sooner *lived to study* than his life was assailed by more dreadful calamities, disease and insanity."

The concluding pages of Johnson's biography contain clarifications of his original assessments in the "Character" of Collins. Johnson records a final visit the Wartons made to Collins in Chichester, and their admiration of the previously unknown "ode inscribed to Mr. John Hume, on the superstitions of the Highlands; which they thought superior to his other works, but which no search has yet found." The mention of this visit is then followed by further remarks on Collins's disorder, which Johnson now perceives not as "alienation of mind, but general laxity and feebleness, a deficiency rather of his vital than intellectual powers." Johnson notes Collins's understandable attempt to snatch "that temporary relief with which the table and the bottle flatter and seduce" as his dreadful malady became more burdensome to him. He concludes his life, however, with several specific and highly stringent remarks on Collins's poetry: he finds his diction harsh and labored; he believes that Collins "affected the obsolete when it was not worthy of revival"; he criticizes lines that are commonly of slow motion, and, perhaps more tellingly, refuses to condone Collins's idiosyncratic syntax.

What we witness in these final remarks is Johnson's attempt to judge Collins's work within the canons of English poetry that are at the heart of his *Lives of the Poets.*[16] Clearly the eighteen years that passed between the publication of the brief sketch in the *Poetical Calendar* and the preparation of a fuller assessment for the *Lives* only strengthened Johnson's belief that Collins's poetic achievement suffered in its isolation from — or rebellion against — the major tradition of Augustan verse. Collins is ultimately judged almost as harshly as is Gray, and it is probable that Johnson also had Gray in mind when he wrote that Collins "puts his words out of the common order, seeming to think, with some later candidates for fame, that not to write prose is certainly to write poetry." But there is always a personal note in Johnson's "Life of Collins" that finally distinguishes it from the "Life of Gray." Johnson opens this final section by lamenting, "Such was the fate of Collins, with whom I once delighted to converse, and whom I yet remember with tenderness," and he closes it by observing, "As men are often esteemed who cannot be loved, so the poetry of Collins may sometimes extort praise when it gives little pleasure." Johnson's affection for the friend of his early years in London remained undiminished; in the year following the publication of the "Life of Collins," Johnson, on vacation in Brighton, had his friend Metcalf carry him to Chichester so that he could view the city in which Collins had been born.[17]

II

A collation of the many printings of Johnson's text casts additional light on the making of his "Life of Collins." Hampton's and Johnson's "Account" was reprinted three times in 1764: in a second edition of the *Poetical Calendar,* and in the pages of the *Gentleman's Magazine* and the *Monthly Review.*[18] Johnson's "Character" was later reprinted in *Miscellaneous and Fugitive Pieces* (1773), which collected many of Johnson's scattered works. This collection was published by Thomas Davies while Johnson was absent from London, and although Boswell records that Johnson "was at first very angry, as he had good reason to be," he "soon relented, and continued his kindness to him as formerly."[19] Johnson's "Character" next appeared as part of the expanded life of Collins in the *Prefaces,* issued in 1781. Neither Johnson's original manuscript of the "Character" nor his later manuscript additions have survived, but two sets of proof-sheets of the "Preface," corrected by Johnson and John Nichols, are preserved in the Victoria and Albert Museum, and they contain important material concerning the evolution of Johnson's text. The "Preface" to Collins's work was reprinted the same year in *The Lives of the Most Eminent English Poets; With Critical Observations on their Works.* A third edition of the *Lives,* the last to receive Johnson's corrections, appeared in 1783.

The following collation table records all substantive variants appearing in each reprinting of Johnson's "Character" and "Life of Collins," as well as all accidental variants appearing in the proof-sheets and subsequent editions. For purposes of clarity, page and line numbers refer to the final edition (*Lives* 1783).

The reprinting of Johnson's "Character" of Collins in the *Gentleman's Magazine* introduced only two substantive variants: "nor" for "not" (possibly a simple misprint) and "to school" for "to the school." Neither change is to be found in the proof-sheets of the "Preface," and we can therefore be fairly certain that this version of the "Character" was not used as copy for the expanded life. This printing of the "Character" also differs in several places in its accidentals — especially in the addition of italics — but there is no reason to think that Johnson had any hand in these changes, which are uniform with printing practices in the *Gentleman's Magazine.* The reprinting of the "Character" in the *Monthly Review* does not introduce any substantive variants into the text, and the changes in accidentals that occur here are not followed in the proof-sheets of the "Preface."

We might naturally assume that Johnson simply used the text of his original "Character" of Collins in the *Poetical Calendar* when he prepared his more ambitious "Preface" for the printer in 1781. A comparison of this text with the proof-sheets reveals very few substantive variants, and the many changes in accidentals that appear in the proof-sheets are almost certainly the work of the printer, who was expected to normalize Johnson's copy. But the table of variants demonstrates that this assumption is actually false: the two substantive variants that appear in the proof-sheets have their origin in the text published in *Miscellaneous and Fugitive Pieces* (2: 237-239). This text is based, in turn, on the *Poetical Calendar* (it does not follow the variants introduced in the *Gentleman's Magazine*); the two substantive variants it does introduce ("on in his" for "on his" and "writing" for "waiting") are both mistakes that found their way into the proof-sheets of 1781. The first mistake was apparently changed by the printer after the proof-sheets had been read by Johnson (who substituted a longer word — "perceived" for "found" — in this line); the second was corrected by Johnson himself. It therefore appears that Johnson, when searching for a copy of his original "Character," ironically turned to the corrupt version appearing in a publication he had not authorized. Perhaps of even greater interest (as I shall explain later) is Johnson's use of a text that included only his "Character" (Hampton's account was not reprinted in Davies's publication).

The text of the "Character" in *Miscellaneous and Fugitive Pieces* also raises questions about the establishment of Johnson's accidentals. The text of 1773 introduces major changes in punctuation, capitalization, and italics, changes that do not follow those found in the *Gentleman's Magazine* or the *Monthly*

No.	page: line (1783)	Poetical Calendar 1763	Gentleman's Magazine 1764	Miscellaneou. and Fugitive Pieces 1773
1	309:11			
2	310:9			
3	310:13			
4	310:19			
5	311:1			
6	311:12			
7	311:12			
8	311:14			
9	311:20			
10	311:23			
11	312:2			
12	312:4			
13	312:5–6			
14	313:3	But	~	~
15	313:13	nor	not	nor
16	314:17–18	found	~	~
17	314:18	on his	~	on in his*
18	314:24	Colchester	~	~
19	314:24	at last	~	~
20	315:3	waiting	~	writing
21	315:6	had then	~	~
22	315:9	to the school	to school	to the schoc
23	315:12	says	~	~
24	315:17			
25	315:17			
26	315:21			
27	316:9–10			

[+]this correction is made by Nichols in Proof "A" and by a third hand in Proof "C

*this text also misprints "interlects" for "intellects"

**this correction is possibly not in Johnson's hand

Proof "C" of *Preface* 1781	Johnson's MS. alterations on Proof "C"	*Prefaces* 1781	*Lives* 1781	*Lives* 1783
the	—	the	*The*	~
not,	*comma deleted*	not	~	~
planned	designed	~	~	~
historical	remote	~	~	~
however	from time to time (*deleted*); now and then	now-and-then	~	~
translator	—	translation[+]	~	~
poetick works	Poeticks	~	~	~
money, which	as much money as	~	~	~
nothing	not live	~	~	~
happiness.	—	~ .	~ .	~ ,
by disease	—	disease	~	~
when	while	~	~	~
now insert it	insert it here	~	~	~
~	Yet as	~	~	~
~	—	~	~	~
~	perceived	~	~	~
~	—	on his	~	~
~	Chichester	~	~	~
~	—	in 1756	~	~
~	waiting	~	~	~
~	then *deleted*	had	~	~
~	—	~	~	~
~	—	~	~	said
no paragraph	*new paragraph noted*	*new paragraph*	~	~
was once visited	once *deleted*	was visited	~	~
Afiatick	Asiatick**	~	~	~
couch: a	—	couch, till a	~	~

Review. Some — but not all — of these changes in accidentals are followed in the proof-sheets of the "Preface," which suggests that punctuation really began anew in 1781 — when copy for the "Character" was combined with the author's manuscript of the expanded sections for the "Preface" — and was either the work of the printer or (less likely) of Johnson himself. A comparison of the proof-sheets with the texts of 1763 and 1773 reveals, moreover, that the incorrect mention of "Colchester" as the place of Collins's death was not altered before it reached proof; and if Johnson did not bother to correct an obvious mistake at this stage it is not likely that he gave any attention at all to refinements in punctuation. It was often Johnson's practice to reserve correction and revision until his manuscript appeared in proof, and this seems to be the case with the "Life of Collins."[20]

Two copies of the proof-sheets have survived. The first, an incomplete set, includes pages 1-6 and 11-14 (cited as "A" and "B" by Fleeman).[21] It is not clear whether Johnson read through this copy; the only writing in his hand appears in the right margin of the first page: "The author is much obligd to Mr Nicol for his help in dates. &c." This copy was obviously meant for John Nichols, one of the booksellers in the consortium that commissioned the *Prefaces* and, as the sole printer of the first edition, Johnson's most important associate in the preparation of the text. Johnson in fact relied upon Nichols for information throughout the writing of the *Lives,* and intended Nichols to fill in several blanks in the manuscript (and even in the proof-sheets) of some of his biographies.[22] Nichols's hand occurs at three points in proof-sheets A and B. At the foot of the first page Nichols wrote: "There is no mention when Mr Collins died. It was in 1756 at Chichester" (I shall return to this entry later). On the fourth page of proofs, Nichols corrected the printer's "translator" to "translation," and on page 11 he altered "Afiatick" to "Asiatick" (this correction is also made, possibly by Johnson, in his copy). The only other change in this set of proofs ("nothing" is correctly altered to "not live" on page 5) is made by a third hand, apparently the same hand that also appears in proof-sheet C.

Johnson's corrections and revisions occur throughout proof-sheet C, a complete set that he clearly examined carefully before returning to Nichols. His corrections, in addition to those already noted, include Aristotle's "Poeticks" for "poetick works," "Chichester" for "Colchester," and "waiting" for "writing." Johnson also noted that a new paragraph should begin with the account of the Wartons' visit to Collins in Chichester, and he therefore indicated an indentation at this point and the deletion of a word ("once"). This appears to raise a textual problem, however, for it is not clear whether Johnson would have removed the word if an indentation had not been required here. Johnson was aware of the heavy costs involved in making substantial alterations in type;[23] but, on the other hand, he made a similar deletion of "then" on the previous page. His only other correction is the deletion of a comma (no. 2 in the collation table).

Johnson's revisions appear most frequently in the passages that supplement the original "Character." For the most part, these alterations are consistent with Johnson's characteristic avoidance of repetition of words or unevenness of cadence.[24] Thus "But" is changed to "Yet as" because "but" had already appeared in the previous line, and "I shall now insert it" is altered to "I shall insert it here" for greater smoothness. Occasionally Johnson's revisions provide an increased precision in his parallel constructions: "historical" is changed to "remote enquiries" as a more appropriate pairing with "abstracted meditations" (repetition may have been a factor here as well, however, for Johnson was to speak of Collins's *History of the Revival of Learning* in the following line). At one point Johnson's alteration of "he did nothing to exhaust" to "he did not live to exhaust" is clarified in another hand (the third hand that appears in proof-sheet A). There is an additional correction in this hand (no. 6), as well as instructions (apparently by a fourth hand) for the printer to adjust several lines of type in the closing pages of this set of proofs.

The text of the life in the *Prefaces* of 1781 reveals a generally faithful adherence to Johnson's corrected proof-sheets, but several of the variants introduced in this text do raise questions about the role of Nichols and his associates. At one point in proof-sheet C, for example, Johnson examined the ironies of Collins's inheritance by pointing out that he was soon "assailed by more dreadful calamities, by disease and insanity." In the *Prefaces,* however, the passage reads "assailed by more dreadful calamities, disease and insanity." It might be argued that this change — like others throughout the corrected proofs — eliminates unnecessary repetition, but there is no surviving evidence to suggest that Johnson was actually responsible for this change. A similar textual dilemma occurs later in the life, when Johnson speaks of the Wartons' visit to Chichester: the original reading in the proof-sheets ("he was forced to rest upon the couch: a short cessation restored his powers") appears as "he was forced to rest upon the couch, till a short cessation" in the *Prefaces* text. Clearly Nichols (or his associates in the printing-house) were responsible for at least one correction at this stage (no. 17) as well as one modification in accidentals (no. 5), and it is quite possible that this alteration of substantives was also their work.

Only one additional variant in the "Life of Collins" appeared when the ten-volume *Prefaces* of 1779-81 was reissued in the format of the four-volume *Lives* in 1781. Boswell records that Johnson received a "bonus" of one hundred pounds when the *Prefaces* was completed, and an additional one hundred pounds for a few corrections when the *Lives* was first published.[25] David Fleeman cites corrections that were made in several of the lives for this publication, but it is doubtful whether the variant introduced in the "Life of Collins" ("the *Gentleman's Magazine*" became *"The Gentleman's Magazine"*) can be considered an authorial correction.[26] Johnson did, however, complete a more extensive revision of the text for the third edition (*Lives* 1783), but it is still difficult to determine whether the variants occurring in that text were actually authorized by Johnson. One of the two variants in the "Life of Collins" is clearly an error in printing (no. 10: the period closing a sentence is replaced by a comma). The other variant ("said Collins" for "says Collins") is consistent with Johnson's tendency in the corrected proofsheets to eliminate vague temporal indicators ("once," "then"), but there is no external evidence to corroborate this speculation. Moreover, the volume entitled *The Principal Additions and Corrections in the Third Edition of Dr. Johnson's Lives of the Poets; collected to complete The Second Edition* does not include any revisions for the "Life of Collins."

I I I

An examination of the different stages of Johnson's text poses several general questions that have a bearing both on Johnson's practice as a biographer and on textual issues throughout the *Lives.* How, for example, are we to determine whether Johnson authorized substantive variants that were introduced at several different points in the transmission of the text? We may accept the printer's correction of obvious errors as consistent with Johnson's general concern for an accurate text, but the substantive changes that occur in at least two stages of the "Life of Collins" (*Prefaces* 1781 and *Lives* 1783) alert us to the considerable gaps in our knowledge of the printing of Johnson's *Lives*.

The determination of a copy-text poses similar problems, even though the survival of Johnson's proof-sheets for many of the lives clarifies much of the confusion here. Birkbeck Hill followed the 1783 text in his edition because it represented "the last edition published in Johnson's lifetime."[27] Modern editors would certainly ascribe more authority to the first edition, however, and the existence of Johnson's proof-sheets allows us to gauge that edition's accuracy with some confidence. The substantial accuracy of the text of the "Life of Collins" in the *Prefaces* has been established, and it is clear that Johnson gave Nichols wide discretionary powers in the matter of accidentals and last-minute additions. Hilles argues that questions concerning spelling, capitalization, and punctuation in the "Life of Pope" were left entirely to the printer,[28] and this seems to be true of both stages in the printing of the "Life of Collins" (i.e., both in the printing of proof-sheets for *Prefaces* 1781 from Johnson's manuscript and *Miscellaneous and Fugitive Pieces*, and in additional corrections and the later alteration of accidentals following Johnson's revisions). We can safely conclude that Johnson tacitly relied upon Nichols (and Nichols's printer) to standardize his accidentals, even though Johnson might later inspect them rigorously himself and make further changes if he thought them necessary (see nos. 2 and 24). The examination of revised proof seemed unnecessary to him, as he explained to Nichols in a letter of 26 October 1780: "I think you never need send back the revises unless something important occurs. Little things, if I omit them, you will do me the favour of setting right yourself."[29] The text of the *Prefaces* of 1781 therefore appears to provide the most satisfactory copy-text for the "Life of Collins," and surely for most of the other lives as well.

Johnson's mention of these "Little things" raises specific questions, however, about Nichols's role in the making of the "Life of Collins." As we have already seen, Hampton incorrectly reported that Collins died in 1756. Hampton was apparently out of touch with Collins by the time the poet had retired to Chichester, and it is not surprising (given the confusion surrounding Collins's illness) that Collins's other friends were also unable to provide a correct date for his death. Johnson did not specify a date in the proof-sheets of the "Preface"; his original "Character" merely referred to "Colchester, where death at last came to his relief," and he corrected the place of death without inserting a date. There are at least two possible reasons for Johnson's omission: either he did not accept Hampton's date, or he simply did not realize that his own account lacked this piece of information. It seems doubtful that he rejected Hampton's date, however, for "in 1756" was inserted in the text of the "Preface" and was not removed in either the second or third edition. It thus appears that Johnson simply forgot to add this detail to his life, as Nichols noted: "There is no mention when Mr Collins died. It was in 1756 in Chichester." And the most probable reason for Johnson's forgetfulness seems to lie in his choice of the *Miscellaneous and Fugitive Pieces* text as copy for his "Character" (Davies's collection did not print Hampton's half of their combined account). It appears that Nichols, wishing to supplement Johnson's sketch, discovered a copy of the *Poetical Calendar* and thereby introduced the incorrect date into this and subsequent editions.[30]

A similar problem is raised by the inclusion of Collins's poem "To Miss Aurelia C—r" at the conclusion of Johnson's life. This short poem was first attributed to Collins by Hampton, who printed the poem in his "Account." But Johnson, writing to Nichols in early 1780, complained: "Dr. Warton tells me that Collins's first piece is in the G:M: for August, 1739. In August there is no such thing. *Amasius* was at that time the poetical name of Dr *Swan* who translated Sydenham. Where to find Collins I know not."[31] It is not clear whether Warton was referring to this poem (published in the January issue) or to Collins's "Sonnet," which was printed with one of Warton's poems in the October issue; in either case, Johnson was understandably confused when he failed to find the poem in the magazine for August. Johnson was also confused by the *Gentleman's* attribution of the poem to Amasius, for he knew that Dr. John Swan regularly used that pseudonym in submitting his poems. Johnson would have discovered a solution to this problem had he noticed a small clarification following the poetical essays in January: *"The two Poems sign'd Amasius in this Mag. are from different Correspondents."*[32]

The dilemma, however, appears to have been placed in Nichols's hands, and it seems probable that Nichols discovered the poem where he also found the (incorrect) date of Collins's death: both sets of proof-sheets of the "Preface" include Collins's poem and announce that this "first production is added here from the *Poetical Calendar.*" It is possible, of course, that Johnson was responsible for rediscovering this poem; and it is clear, at least, that he approved of its inclusion in the life — even as an afterthought — for he allowed it to stand in the proof-sheets and later editions. But it is more likely that the poem was discovered by Nichols, whose more deferential voice appears to introduce the uncharacteristically formal "Mr." into the description of Collins's first poem.[33]

The situation is certainly a complicated one, but the following sequence can be determined fairly clearly. Johnson appears not to have consulted a copy of the *Poetical Calendar* before he queried Nichols about the publication of Collins's first poem. Collation of the proof-sheets with the text of Johnson's "Character" in *Miscellaneous and Fugitive Pieces* also demonstrates that Johnson was not relying upon the original text of the "Character" when he prepared the expanded life for the printer in 1781. "To Miss Aurelia C — r" was added to the life in the proof-sheets, however, but its placement at the conclusion suggests that either Johnson or Nichols (probably the latter) finally turned to the *Poetical Calendar* only after the rest of the manuscript was ready for the printer. Johnson apparently accepted this addition to his life, but in revising the proof-sheets he did not notice that the date of Collins's death was also lacking in his final sketch. Nichols, noting this omission in his own copy of the proofs, added the date before the "Preface" was printed, and it is almost certain that his source was Hampton's "Account" in the *Poetical Calendar*. Johnson, who thanked Nichols for his "help in dates" on proof-sheet A, allowed the date to stand in subsequent editions of the life.

This reconstruction of the preparation of Johnson's life helps explain some obvious discrepancies between Hampton's "Account" and Johnson's final version. We have already seen how closely Johnson appears to echo Hampton's sketch, especially in his opening paragraph; but there are several points at which Johnson does not make full use of the information Hampton provides. Johnson adds Collins's birthday, for example, but he substitutes "about 1720" for Hampton's more definite "1721." Johnson also thanks Joseph Warton for informing him that Collins was admitted a scholar of Winchester "in 1733," whereas Hampton (who was also Collins's schoolfellow) had provided an exact date: "Feb. 23, 1733."[34] Hampton also supplied a date for Collins's election to a demyship at Magdalen, whereas Johnson simply states that he was elected a demy "about half a year" after he arrived at Queen's as a commoner. Hampton, moreover, believed that Collins left Oxford because he was "weary of the confinement and uniformity of an academical life"; Johnson, however, merely writes that Collins "suddenly left the University; for what reason I know not that he told."

It was Johnson's usual practice, as several scholars have shown, to make full use of earlier biographical accounts when he prepared his own *Lives of the Poets*.[35] The major discrepancies noted here, however, suggest that Johnson did not consistently draw upon Hampton's biographical sketch of Collins, even though his own "Character" appeared as part of it when it was first published in 1763. There is actually little — if any — information in the final "Life of Collins" that Johnson could not have received from Joseph Warton (or from Nichols); and it thus seems likely that these occasional echoes were produced by Johnson's recollection of Hampton's memoir rather than by an actual recasting of it. What may finally strike us as most unusual in Johnson's preparation of the "Life of Collins" is not only his recourse to a corrupt text of his "Character" (printed in an unauthorized collection of his works), but his reliance, as well, upon a version of his original sketch that, without Hampton's memoir, lacked the very information he was forced to search for elsewhere.

NOTES

1. For a discussion of their collaboration, see my introduction to Warton's *Odes on Various Subjects* (Los Angeles: Augustan Reprint Society, 1979). As I make clear later, Warton provided information to Johnson for his "Life of Collins."

2. Although copies of the *Poetical Calendar* are rare, the "Account" has been reprinted in *Early Biographical Writings of Dr. Johnson,* introd. J.

D. Fleeman (Westmead, Hants.: Gregg International, 1973), pp. 513-518. The "Account" originally appeared on pp. 107-112 of the *Poetical Calendar*. Throughout this essay I refer to Johnson's original sketch of 1763 as his "Character" of Collins in order to distinguish it from the expanded "Preface" that appeared in the first edition of the *Lives of the English Poets* (*Prefaces* 1781) and, as the "Life of Collins," in the second and third editions (*Lives* 1781 and *Lives* 1783).

3. Hester Lynch Piozzi, *Anecdotes of the Late Samuel Johnson, LL.D.*, ed. Arthur Sherbo (London: Oxford Univ. Press, 1974), p. 75.

4. See A. T. Hazen and T. O. Mabbott, "Dr. Johnson and Francis Fawkes's Theocritus," *RES* 21 (1945): 142-146, and Arthur Sherbo, "Dr. Johnson's 'Judicious Remarks,'" *JNL* 19, no. 1 (1959): 10. Johnson's name is also on the list of subscribers to Fawkes's *Original Poems* (1761); see *A Bibliography of Samuel Johnson*, ed. William Prideaux Courtney and David Nichol Smith (Oxford: Clarendon Press, 1915; rpt. 1968), p. 102.

5. *GM* 51 (Jan. 1781): 11-12.

6. *Literary Magazine*, 1 (1756): 39.

7. *GM* 44 (Oct. 1774): 525.

8. *GM* 44 (Dec. 1774): 627.

9. *The Correspondence and Other Papers of James Boswell Relating to the Making of the "Life of Johnson,"* ed. Marshall Waingrow (New York: McGraw-Hill, 1969), p. 8. Afterwards cited as "Waingrow."

10. Ibid., p. 231 and n. 3.

11. *Boswell's Life of Johnson*, ed. G. B. Hill, rev. L. F. Powell (Oxford: Clarendon Press, 1934-50), 1: 22, 382-383.

12. *Letters to Gilbert White of Selborne from . . . the Rev. John Mulso*, ed. R. Holt-White (London: Porter [1907]), p. 188.

13. For a full analysis of Collins's illness — and Johnson's attempts to define it — see my article "'Poor Collins' Reconsidered," *HLQ* 42 (1979): 91-116.

14. *The Letters of Samuel Johnson*, ed. R. W. Chapman (Oxford: Clarendon Press, 1952), 1:53, 60, 90. Afterwards cited as *Letters*.

15. I quote from the first edition (*Prefaces* 1781).

16. For discussions of the relationship between biography and criticism in the *Lives*, see Lawrence Lipking, *The Ordering of the Arts in Eighteenth-Century England* (Princeton: Princeton Univ. Press, 1970), pp. 405-462, and Robert Folkenflik's recent study, *Samuel Johnson, Biographer* (Ithaca: Cornell Univ. Press, 1978), chs. 6 and 7. Johnson's antagonism towards Gray is admirably analyzed by Roger Lonsdale, "Gray and Johnson: The Biographical Problem," in *Fearful Joy: Papers from the Thomas Gray Bicentenary Conference at Carleton University*, ed. James Downey and Ben Jones (Montreal: McGill-Queen's Univ. Press, 1974), pp. 66-84.

17. Waingrow, p. 589.

18. *GM* 34 (Jan. 1764): 23-24; *MR* 30 (Feb. 1764): 120-122. The second edition of the *Poetical Calendar* is extremely rare. The *British Museum General Catalogue of Printed Books* (71:440) states that vols. 3, 4, 5, 8, and 9 are of the second edition (and that vol. 3 is dated 1764), but I have not been able to locate a copy of the second edition of vol. 12.

19. *Boswell's Life of Johnson*, 2:271.

20. See Frederick W. Hilles, "The Making of *The Life of Pope*," in *New Light on Dr. Johnson*, ed. Hilles (New Haven: Yale Univ. Press, 1959), pp. 281-282. Afterwards cited as "Hilles."

21. J. D. Fleeman, "Some Proofs of Johnson's *Prefaces to the Poets*," *The Library* 5th ser., 17 (1962): 213-230 (esp. p. 228). Afterwards cited as "Fleeman." The proof-sheets of the "Life of Collins" are Forster 298-48-D-56, 57.

22. Hilles, p. 277. Edward Hart, "Some New Sources of Johnson's *Lives*," *PMLA* 65 (1950): 1088-1111, also comments on Nichols's assistance.

23. *Letters*, 1: 417-418 (to William Strahan).

24. See, for example, Hilles, p. 275, and Fleeman, p. 227.

25. *Boswell's Life of Johnson,* 4:35 and n. 3.

26. Fleeman, p. 214 and n. 1. Clarence Tracy, in his edition of the *Life of Savage* (Oxford: Clarendon Press, 1971), pp. xxxiv-xxxv, states that no new readings in this biography are "certainly authorial" in *Lives* 1781.

27. Samuel Johnson, *Lives of the English Poets,* ed. George Birkbeck Hill (Oxford: Clarendon Press, 1905), 1: vii (the phrase is from Harold Spencer Scott's account of his uncle's practice).

28. Hilles, p. 278.

29. *Letters,* 2:407.

30. It could also be argued that Nichols's note was intended for Johnson, who then offered Nichols his thanks; but, because Johnson did not subsequently add this date to either set of proofs, it still seems likely that the change was later made by Nichols. J. P. Hardy, in his edition of Johnson's *Lives of the Poets: A Selection* (Oxford: Clarendon Press, 1971), p. 366, also notes that Nichols was responsible for this incorrect date, but he does not indicate that the source for it lay in Hampton's half of the "Account." (This source is also neglected by Herman W. Liebert, "Johnson's Revisions," *JNL* 11, no. 2 [1951]: 7.) Hardy also states (p. 365) that Johnson was "doubtless indebted for some details of the poet's life" to Hampton's "Account," but I suggest that this is probably not true.

31. *Letters,* 2:332-333.

32. *GM* 9 (Jan. 1739): 43. For a full account of the confusion surrounding this poem, see *The Works of William Collins,* ed. Richard Wendorf and Charles Ryskamp (Oxford: Clarendon Press, 1979), pp. 99-101.

33. Johnson refers to his friend as "Collins" throughout the life with one exception, when he quotes directly from his "Character."

34. Hampton provides the old-style date; Collins was actually admitted to Winchester in 1734.

35. See, for example, Hilles, pp. 263-267; Lipking, *The Ordering of the*

Arts, pp. 422-428; James H. Leicester, "Johnson's Life of Shenstone: Some Observations on the Sources," *Johnsonian Studies*, ed. Magdi Wahba (Cairo: privately printed, 1962), pp. 189-222; Wayne Warncke, "Samuel Johnson on Swift: The *Life of Swift* and Johnson's Predecessors in Swiftian Biography," *JBS* 7 (1968): 56-64; and Hilbert H. Campbell, "Shiels and Johnson: Biographers of Thomson," *SEL* 12 (1972): 535-544.

Chapter 8
Robert Dodsley as Editor

I N SPITE OF THE considerable amount of bibliographical
work that has been devoted to Robert Dodsley and his
Collection of Poems, surprisingly little attention has been
paid to Dodsley's role as an editor of eighteenth-century
poetry.[1] That an examination of editorial influence should
focus on Dodsley is natural for several reasons. He was, after all,
the doyen of mid-eighteenth-century London publishers. It was
Johnson who paid tribute to Dodsley's treatment of authors by
claiming that "Doddy, you know, is my patron."[2] In an age in
which literary patronage had largely been abandoned by the
aristocracy, it was to the publisher (and former footman) Dodsley that "literary adventurers" like Johnson and Collins
addressed themselves. Much information about Dodsley has

This essay represents my first attempt to investigate editorial practices and
house style in eighteenth-century printing history. It was published in *Studies in Bibliography* 31 (1978): 235-248. Since then, three important studies or
editions of Dodsley have appeared: *The Correspondence of Robert Dodsley
1733-1764*, ed. James E. Tierney (Cambridge: Cambridge Univ. Press, 1988);
Harry M. Solomon, *The Rise of Robert Dodsley: Creating the New Age of
Print* (Carbondale and Edwardsville: Southern Illinois Univ. Press, 1996);
and Robert Dodsley, *A Collection of Poems by Several Hands*, introd.
Michael F. Suarez (London: Routledge/Thoemmes Press, 1997).

fortunately survived, some of it through the care of the poet William Shenstone, who preserved the vigorous correspondence between himself and his good friend. The evidence itself, however, is often contradictory and points to Dodsley's peculiar position as editor, publisher, and self-taught man of letters. It is clear that Dodsley took considerable care in preparing his authors' works for the press; whether he in fact took too much care in some cases is a question closely related to his editorial zeal and to his own conception of himself as poet and dramatist. The substantive readings of his poets' texts were often altered when they appeared in the *Collection,* and their accidentals almost always modified to agree with its distinctive "house style." The following observations, although they should provide a much more substantial portrait of Dodsley as editor, are offered in the expectation that, in answering some questions, they will raise others.

Of Dodsley's publications, *A Collection of Poems by Several Hands* (1748-58) is of primary importance in determining the kinds of influence the bookseller could have had on poetical texts. The *Collection* itself is a major document in eighteenth-century taste, a diverse mixture of poetry in which Pope was accompanied by Tickell, Johnson by Chesterfield, Collins by Stephen Duck.[3] It was Dodsley's purpose, as he stated in the "Advertisement" to the first edition, "to preserve to the Public those poetical performances, which seemed to merit a longer remembrance, than what would probably be secured to them by the MANNER wherein they were originally published" (1:1). Many of the poems in the miscellany, moreover, were offered to the public for the first time. Gray's "Ode on the Spring" and "Ode on the Death of a Favourite Cat" were transmitted to Dodsley by Horace Walpole, a common friend, and they first appeared anonymously in the *Collection* in 1748.

The five poems by Collins that appeared in the first and fourth volumes, however, had already been published in his *Odes* or in *An Epistle: Address to Sir Thomas Hanmer*, but it was Dodsley who was responsible for keeping these poems in print until Collins's work was collected in 1763 and 1765. The age owed to these volumes, more than to anything else, R. W. Chapman has written, "its knowledge of some poems which are still famous. Gray's poems were not collected in a popular form until 1768, Johnson's not until 1785," Chapman continues, "but *The Vanity of Human Wishes*, the *Drury-Lane Prologue*, and some of Gray's *Odes* were universally accessible because they were in Dodsley. If this were not borne in mind, the bibliographical evidence would suggest that the *Vanity*, like the Eton *Ode* and Collins's *Ode to Evening*, must have been almost forgotten for twenty years or more."[4]

In selecting the poems for his *Collection*, Dodsley was influenced by settled reputation as well as by the opinion of literary middle-men like Walpole, Shenstone, and Joseph Spence. According to W. P. Courtney, who compiled a book-length study of Dodsley's miscellany, "Most of the pieces composing these volumes were submitted to the judgment of George, the first Lord Lyttelton, before they were passed for printing. . . . Many poems were inserted in the third and the later volumes from members of New College, Oxford, who had passed through their school education at Winchester College, and these were probably supplied through Spence, Dodsley's warm friend for many years, and a member of both these establishments."[5]

According to Dodsley's biographer Ralph Straus, much of the success of the *Collection* was in fact due to "Dodsley's personal friendships with the authors, and to their active assistance."[6] Dodsley's correspondence during the years of the *Collection* is filled with his attempts to charm, cajole, or reason

his authors into the kind of assistance he needed. Intent on publishing Shenstone's elegies, Dodsley wrote: "Upon my word, Sir,
if you do not bring me up these mourning Muses, nothing elegant will come from Tully's Head this season. I shall loose the
Fame of being the Muses' Midwife, & my hand for want of practice will forget its obstetrick faculties" (BL Add. MS. 28959, f.
49). Poor Dodsley, Straus writes, "was at times hard put to it to
keep his temper with his scattered band of poets" (p. 103), especially when he experienced difficulty in retrieving proof from
leisurely authors like his friend Shenstone. Dodsley wrote to
Shenstone in 1758, concerning volumes five and six of the *Collection:* "I had expected every day for some time to have receiv'd
the two remaining Sheets from You, when behold another Letter came without a Proof! Ah, dear M.r Shenstone! consider
what a sad situation I am in — big with *twins,* at my *full time,*
and no hopes of your assistance to *deliver* me! Was ever *man* in
such a situation before?" (BL Add. MS. 28959, f. 92).

But the poets themselves, as their letters to each other attest,
were often hard pressed to keep their tempers with Dodsley, and
it is this kind of friction between bookseller and writer that
allows us a closer view of Dodsley's editorial practices. The
poets asserted that Dodsley not only chose to print what he
wanted, but sometimes altered their poems as well, an alteration
of substantives that obviously has a direct bearing on several
important mid-century poetical texts. Although information
does not survive concerning each of the contributors to Dodsley's miscellany, it is nevertheless possible to clarify Dodsley's
editorial policy by analyzing his treatment of the poets Dyer,
Gray, and Shenstone.[7]

The country clergyman John Dyer had two poems, "Grongar
Hill" and "The Ruins of Rome," published in the first edition of
Dodsley's *Collection* (1748).[8] Dyer, an ill man by 1756, still had

hopes that his poem *The Fleece* might be accepted by Dodsley, although he admitted that "people are so taken up with politics, and have so little inclination to read anything but satire and newspapers, I am in doubt whether this is a proper time for publishing it." Nevertheless, with the assistance and enthusiasm of Mark Akenside and Joseph Warton, Dyer sent the poem on to Dodsley and it was published 15 March 1757. In a letter to a friend, Dyer recorded his reaction to the edition: "Mr Dodsley, I think, has performed his part well; but in one or two places there have happened such alterations of the copy, as make me give my reader false precepts. . . . I will not trouble you with any . . . corrections, but I will Mr Dodsley, lest a second edition should happen." In his letter to Dodsley, Dyer pointed out the mistakes caused by Dodsley's ignorance of the methods of "us graziers," and expressed his hope that "these remarks will be agreeable to you. If you are inclined to make use of them, or any others, which I may send you, be pleased to acquaint me." Dyer died in December, however, and a corrected edition of *The Fleece* was never published.

Dodsley's treatment of *The Fleece* prompted Straus to note "that on several occasions Dodsley seems to have trusted his own judgment and sense of rhythm rather than the manuscript given to him for publication. That he was justified in such a course is open to question, but one may imagine him reading to a circle of friends the latest parcel to arrive, and then and there pencilling such alterations as seemed to please the company" (p. 110). But whereas Dodsley and his company may have been pleased with the alterations, a man like Dyer, whose poem was in part a technical treatise (on sheep-raising and the wool trade), had reason to complain at his falsified "precepts," even though Dodsley himself was a poet with a considerable reputation in the 1740s.

Gray's immediate reaction to the *Collection* was not to any changes Dodsley might have made in the printing of his poems but to the aesthetic appearance of the miscellany itself. In January or February 1748 he wrote to Walpole: "I am obliged to you for Mr. Dodsley's book, and, having pretty well looked it over, will (as you desire) tell you my opinion of it. He might, methinks, have spared the Graces in his frontispiece, if he chose to be œconomical, and dressed his authors in a little more decent raiment — not in whited-brown paper and distorted characters, like an old ballad. I am ashamed to see myself; but the company keeps me in countenance."[9] Perhaps as a result of Gray's remarks, Dodsley replaced the three graces that formed the title-page's vignette with one of Apollo and the nine Muses in the second and subsequent editions.

Dodsley had apparently made some alterations to the poems themselves, but Gray makes no mention of these. The two odes ("On the Spring" and "On the Death of a Favourite Cat") had been transmitted to Dodsley by Walpole, who had taken the text from Gray's letters to him. Walpole had already been responsible for getting Gray's "Ode on a Distant Prospect of Eton College" into print (it was published by Dodsley in 1747), and, in his characteristically coy way, Gray seems not to have been averse to having these two other pieces published as well: "As to my Eton Ode, Mr. Dodsley is *padrone*," he wrote to Walpole; "The second you had, I suppose you do not think worth giving him: otherwise, to me it seems not worse than the former. He might have Selima too, unless she be of too little importance for his patriot-collection; or perhaps the *connections* you had with her may interfere. *Che se io?*" (Letter 142).

Gray sent a copy of the "Ode on the Death of a Favourite Cat" to both Walpole (Letter 134) and Thomas Wharton (Letter 135). The Walpole text has not survived, but it is reasonable to believe that it was very similar, but probably not identical, to the text in his letter to Wharton (which differs at several points from the original text in Gray's Commonplace Book). The comparison to be made is therefore between the texts of the poem in the *Collection* and in Gray's letter to Wharton. When "Selima" was inserted into the *Collection,* several noticeable alterations had been made to Gray's manuscript: lines four and five had been transposed; "Her Coat" was changed to "The coat" in line ten; "averse to" in line 24 became "a foe to fish"; and line 36 was changed from "A Fav'rite has no friend!" to "What fav'rite has a friend!" That these changes were apparently Dodsley's responsibility and not Gray's is indicated by later printings of the poem. In *Designs by Mr. R. Bentley for Six Poems by Mr. T. Gray* (Dodsley, 1753) and *Poems by Mr. Gray* (published by James Dodsley in 1768), both of which were supervised by Gray, these changes were replaced by the manuscript readings in the letter to Wharton. These variants were also corrected in later editions of the *Collection,* with the exception of "The coat" in line ten.[10] Much later, when preparing new editions of his poems in 1768, Gray mentioned "several blunders of the press" in Dodsley's previous printings of the poems in the *Collection.*[11]

Gray was not as reticent, however, about Dodsley's handling of his "Elegy Written in a Country Church Yard." Dodsley's printing of the "Elegy" was of course a race against time. Walpole's wide circulation of the poem resulted in a letter from the publisher William Owen to Gray implying that the poem would soon appear in his *Magazine of Magazines.* Faced with this unpleasant prospect, Gray instructed Walpole to offer it to Dodsley: "I have but one bad Way left to escape the Honour they would inflict upon me. & therefore am obliged to desire you would make Dodsley print it immediately (w[ch] may be done in less than a Week's time) from your Copy, but without my Name, in what Form is most convenient for him, but in his best Paper & Character. he must correct the Press himself, & print it without any Interval between the Stanza's, because the Sense is in some Places continued beyond them; & the Title must be, Elegy, wrote in a Country Church-yard" (Letter 157).

And yet in spite of his detailed instructions, Gray was not entirely pleased with Dodsley's publication. He remarked to Walpole (20 February 1751): "Nurse Dodsley has given it a pinch or two in the cradle, that (I doubt) it will bear the marks of as long as it lives. But no matter: we have ourselves suffered under her hands before now; and besides, it will only look the more careless, and by *accident* as it were" (Letter 158). Gray's previous "suffering" clearly points to Dodsley's handling of his odes in the *Collection* three years earlier, and presumably to the miscellany's appearance as well. As for the "pinches" that Dodsley had inflicted this time, Gray made some remarks in a subsequent letter to Walpole: "The chief errata were *sacred* bower for *secret*; *hidden* for *kindred* (in spite of dukes and classicks); and *frowning* as in scorn for *smiling*."[12] These possibly *are* errata: the rapid printing of the poem would aggravate compositors' errors and leave little time for editorial revision. But at the least Dodsley's own contributions appear to be the slight indentation of the first line of each stanza (although he did not separate them), and the addition of the funereal borders of skulls, bones, hourglass, spade, and crown (which were employed through the twelfth edition in 1763).[13]

In his later dealings with Dodsley, Gray often provided specific instructions for his publications that compromised his bookseller's enterprising spirit; Dodsley, however, remained an invariably accommodating publisher. When Gray revised his "Elegy" in 1752, the poet read proof on a publication for the first time (Letter 170). Dodsley wanted to number each stanza in the poem; Gray objected, and the stanzas remained unnumbered. When Dodsley published *Designs by Mr. R. Bentley for Six Poems by Mr. T. Gray* he wanted Gray's name to appear at the top of the title-page, but the poet insisted on the illustrator's pre-eminence and again got his own way (Letter 172). Dodsley also hoped to boost the volume's sales by prefixing the poems with Gray's portrait, but once again the poet remonstrated — this time to Walpole — and the engraving was suppressed (Letter 173). Finally, when Robert's brother James Dodsley, by 1768 the head of the firm, asked Gray if he could bring out a smaller edition of his poems, the poet consented, but with specific instructions: "all I desire is, that the text be accurately printed, & therefore whoever corrects the press, should have some acquaintance with the Greek, Latin, & Italian, as well as the English, tongues" (Letter 465).

In his meticulousness, his pretended indifference to publication, and his distance from the world of London publishing, Gray was in many ways an anomalous contributor to Tully's Head. Gray apparently wrote directly to Dodsley twice only, and met him no oftener.[14] For a fuller view of Dodsley's editorial practice we must look at the career of William Shenstone. Although Shenstone resembled Gray in many ways, especially in his retirement and his attention to literary detail, he was also Dodsley's close friend. In return for the lampreys, porter, and tea that his publisher sent him, Shenstone replied with a steady flow of his own poems and those of his friends, often accompanied by revisions, proof-sheets, and news of his literary circle.

Dodsley published Shenstone's *The Judgment of Hercules* in 1741, and acted as agent for *The School-mistress* the following year. When he was preparing the first three volumes of his *Collection*, Dodsley decided to include *The School-mistress* as it was, taking his copy from the 1742 edition. Shenstone, however, who had apparently been tinkering with his poem for six years, expressed his displeasure to Lady Luxborough: "As to *Dodsley's Collection* I find it is approv'd on all Hands; tho' *I* should have been much better pleas'd with him, if he had giv'n me previous notice e'er he publish'd my Schoolmistress; that I might have *spruc'd her up* a little before she appeared in so much Company. They tell me he purposes a *second* Edition concerning wch I have wrote to him."[15] Shenstone was even more blunt with his friend and fellow poet Richard Jago: "I am afraid, by your account, that Dodsley has published my name to the School-mistress. I was a good deal displeased at his publishing that poem without my knowledge, when he had so many opportunities of giving me some previous information; but, as he would probably disregard my resentment, I chose to stifle it, and wrote to him directly upon the receipt of yours, that I would be glad to furnish him with an improved copy of the School-mistress. &c. for his second edition" (Letter LXIV). In printing from the 1742 edition, Dodsley was of course faithful to his poet's text; all that he failed to take into consideration were his author's altered intentions. Shenstone consulted with his friends Graves, Whistler, and Jago, revised his poem to their mutual satisfaction, and sent it off in time for the second edition.

By 1759, however, Shenstone must have changed his opinion of second editions, for we find Dodsley having to argue rather forcefully on their behalf: "And now I come to your exclamation agst Second Editions, with Additions & Alterations. I shall dispatch this point in a very few words. Would you have an Author, after he has once publish'd, ty'd up from correcting his errors, or improving his Work? Second thoughts you know are said to be the best, & therefore second Editions corrected, are no bad things — I speak as a Bookseller" (BL Add. MS. 28959, f. 115). Dodsley did not, of course, speak just as a bookseller. Perhaps because he was a writer himself, certainly because he understood his authors, he appealed to Shenstone in terms the poet would appreciate; his argument is based not on increased sales but on the improvement of the author's work.

Because they respected Dodsley's poetical integrity, and because they did not have the time themselves, Shenstone and his friends allowed their bookseller an unusual amount of discretion in the final preparation of their poetry for the fourth volume of the *Collection* in 1755. A long letter to Jago, however, shows how uneasy Shenstone was with this arrangement, especially since he was submitting his friends' pieces (as well as his own) to Dodsley's judgment: "I am thoroughly determined never to print any thing for the future, unless I have the company of my friends when I send to the press. Hurried as I then was, I sent up your two copies, and what I proposed for him of my own, with a kind of *discretionary* power to select the best readings. How you would approve of this measure I knew not; but I had this to plead in my behalf, that D[odsley] was a person of taste *himself*; that he had, as I imagined, many learned friends to assist him; that his *interest* was concerned in the perfection of his Miscellany; and that I submitted my own pieces to the same judgement" (Letter CLXXVII). Thus beneath Shenstone's anxiety in the letter we are able to detect his basic trust in Dodsley, another "person of taste," especially in regard to the handling of his own poetry.[16]

Dodsley, for his part, seems to have been as conscientious as Shenstone had hoped: "I have spent this whole day amongst your Papers & those of your friends," he wrote to the poet, "& have put them as nearly in the order you desire as I can. I hope to send you prooft sheets of the whole of them before next week is out, which I beg you will correct & send back by the return of the Post. I have impertinently attempted to alter one Stanza of

Lady Luxborough's, which pray restore to its original reading if you like it better" (BL Add. MS. 28959, ff. 22-23). But Shenstone's uneasiness continued, especially when he corresponded with Lady Luxborough: "I have expected to see Dodsley's miscellany advertis'd these six weeks ago. Had he allow'd me but one *Half* of this time to deliberate, I could have adjusted the share we have in it much more to my satisfaction. I know but little what he has finally done, in pursuance of that discretionary Power with which I, thro' absolute Haste, found it requisite to intrust him; and that possibly at a time when his *own* Hurry was as great as *mine*" (Letter CLXXIX).

Part of Shenstone's trepidation, however, lay in the fact that he too had tampered with Lady Luxborough's verses and was now hoping that Dodsley had restored the original readings: "And if he have *not* done so, *universally* (as I apprehend may be the Case) the Fault may be repair'd in some future Impression, & is, even now, not altogether *mine*" (Letter CLXXIX). Dodsley, on his part, acknowledged his responsibility: "I am in some pain for those different readings which you left so imprudently to my determination but I have done as well as I could, & have generally thought it the best way to follow where you seem'd to point" (BL Add. MS. 28959, f. 37). As late as March 1755 Shenstone wrote to Dodsley in the hope that the edition might be delayed and the verses revised again, but by the twenty-first he had received his copy and was communicating his reaction to Richard Graves: "I wish the last Stanza of WHISTLER's Verses upon Flowers had remained as he himself wrote it: but being somewhat dissatisfied with the original Reading, and having no Time left to improve it myself, I left it to D —— , who I think has made it worse; however, in this Respect, and some others, it may be proper to fix one's Eye upon a subsequent Impression; and

DODSLEY has acted as discreetly as it was possible for him to do, considering what instructions were given him, and how *much* was left to his Discretion" (Letter CLXXXII). Two days later Shenstone acknowledged his receipt of the volume to Dodsley and politely complimented him on his work: "I am oblig'd to you for the care you took to forward it, when printed, as well as for all that Trouble I occasion'd you, *before*. Some Improvements may be made in a subsequent Impression; & whenever this is propos'd I dare say you will give me notice. In general, you have done all that I could expect from a Person of Genius and a Friend" (Letter CLXXXIII).

In spite of his previous anxieties, Shenstone became the principal contributor to (and liaison for) the final two volumes of the *Collection,* published in 1758. In a letter to his friend Thomas Percy, we find that both Shenstone and Dodsley have been tinkering with Percy's contributions; but Shenstone is now more eager to see that Percy himself has the last word: "I recollected that Mr Dodsley & myself had formerly taken some Pains, (and, I believe, some *Liberties* too), with the Pieces to which you alluded. Be this as it will, you are most evidently in ye right for not adopting *implicitly* what was done in your absence; nor can Mr. Dodsley or myself wish to debarr you of a Privilege, which, on a similar occasion, we should be so ready to demand *Ourselves*" (Letter CCXV). In his own dealings with Dodsley, however, Shenstone was now much more willing to trust to his publisher's final judgment: "In regard to the Song 'I told my nymph' I desire y^t you would follow *all* ye readings you propose. (The same, as to ye Compliment 1743.) As to ye Ode 1739. I am neither wholly satisfy'd with y^r reading or my *own*" (Letter CCXIV). Shenstone therefore included both his original first stanza and an altered one and left the final choice to Dodsley.

I.	II.
'Twas not by Beauty's aid alone	'Twas not thro' Beauty's
That Love usurp'd his Fancy'd/	aid alone,
Airy throne,	That Love's insidious pow'r
His fancy'd/magic powr display'd	was known
His tyrant sceptre sway'd	Or ever breast, betray'd
Which &c.	A mutual kindness, &c.

Although Shenstone preferred the altered stanza, Dodsley's final version most closely follows the first and includes several changes of his own:

> 'Twas not by beauty's aid alone,
> That love usurp'd his airy throne,
>   His boasted power display'd:
> 'Tis kindness that secures his aim,
> 'Tis hope that feeds the kindling flame,
>   Which beauty first conveyed. (V, 34)

At this stage Dodsley's and Shenstone's correspondence and their frequent visits together approximate a form of poetical collaboration. If Dodsley supplied the final touches to Shenstone's work, so too Shenstone read and criticized Dodsley's *Melpomene* (1757) and *Cleone* (1759, to which he helped add an epilogue; see Letter CXCVI), and also revised his friend's *Fables* (1761). As a reviser Shenstone placed himself in the same precarious position in which he had formerly found Dodsley: "You will observe, that I take great liberties with the Fables you ask me to revise," he wrote to Graves; "Dodsley must think me *very* fantastical or *worse*, while I was correcting those he wrote at The Leasowes. — I find my *ear* much more apt to take offence than most other people's; and, as *his* is far less delicate than mine, he must of course believe, in many places, that I altered merely for alteration's sake" (Letter CCXLIX). Even Horace Walpole took an active interest in Dodsley's poetry, as he indicated in a letter concerning the unsuccessful *Agriculture*: "I am sorry you think it any trouble to peruse your poem again; I always read it with pleasure. One or two little passages I have taken the liberty to mark and to offer you alterations . . . I don't know whether you will think my emendations for the better. I beg in no wise that you will adopt any of them out of complaisance; I only suggest them to you at your desire, and am far from insisting on them."[17] But *Agriculture,* like Dyer's *The Fleece,* never saw a revised edition.

Thus Dodsley's correspondence with his authors (and Shenstone in particular) reveals how carefully he worked as editor and publisher to obtain the best possible edition for his publications, and to correct errors in earlier editions. Not all of Dodsley's authors were in agreement, of course; Dr. John Brown suggested to Dodsley that "If such a thing is practicable . . . I would have a printed Copy [of *Honour*] sent down by way of Proof, as I cannot expect that You in the hurry of Business should revise it with that Care, as an Author does his own Productions."[18] John Hoadly in fact argued that Dodsley *was* too hurried to present accurate texts of poems in the *Collection:* "I beg the Favour of You to take upon yourself the correct printing of what little pieces of mine there are in it; as they were most shamefully neglected in the last Edition [1755], even to y.ᵉ leaving out whole Lines; to the utter Confusion of Grammar, Sense, and what some Poets might resent more — even Rhime."[19] And in the following month (8 March 1758) Hoadly again reproached his publisher: "I am much surpriz'd to see You advertise, to publish this Month; for except what Pieces you have had corrected by y.ᵉ Authors themselves, (which I think I can plainly trace,) y.ᵉ Volumes are miserably printed. . . . For my sake, let y.ᵉ Pieces taken from my Volumes be corrected; or People will think I don't understand common Grammar" (Bodleian MS. Eng. Letters d. 40, ff. 111-112). But most of Dodsley's authors appear to have agreed with John Gilbert Cooper who, in reference to his essays in *The Museum*, wished that Dodsley "would write it concert with me in the humorous papers, that is, make any addition, altaration, amendment etc as you think proper, for I know nobody's taste I can more rely upon than yours."[20]

The letters of his authors to him, especially when they suggest revisions for Dodsley's own writing, in turn reveal relationships that were founded upon mutual respect. Dodsley's editorial privilege consisted mostly of suggestion; his authors usually had the last word. When they were somewhat displeased with the final results, as Shenstone and his friends were, it was in fact often due to the extensive discretionary power they had put in Dodsley's hands. For Gray, moreover, it was predominantly a comfortable relationship; the discretion (or indiscretion) of Dodsley as *padrone* enabled the poet to indicate his own indifference towards publication. It is clear that this discretionary power often caught Dodsley between the roles of author and publisher. On the one hand, because he was a successful poet and playwright, he was inclined to value (perhaps too highly) his own literary judgment. On the other hand, again because he was an author himself, he maintained respect for a writer's literary property and for the integrity of a literary work. The evidence suggests that Dodsley's band of authors was for the most part pleased with his editorial practice. When Dodsley did alter his writers' texts, as he did Lady Luxborough's, he was usually prompt in pointing out his initiative and asking for approval. And when in fact Dodsley had the final word on any text, his authors could rely on his fierce partisanship for corrected second editions. Dodsley, meanwhile, was clearly open to the suggestions made to him by writers like Gray and Shenstone.

These are substantive changes, however; when we turn to Dodsley's treatment of accidentals we find ourselves on much less solid ground. Although Dodsley can usually be depended upon to preserve his authors' wording (or at least to point to his alterations), his presentation of accidentals often seems to be his own (or that of his compositors).[21] This is particularly true of the *Collection*, which has a distinctive house style that is noticeably different even from Dodsley's earlier and later publications.

We have seen that Dodsley was willing to follow Gray's detailed instructions concerning the substantives of his text, but with the accidentals the bookseller often wished to print for himself.[22] Dodsley's tampering with accidentals is apparent in his presentation of Gray's three poems in the *Collection*. A comparison of Gray's manuscript version of the "Ode on the Spring" in a letter to Walpole with its presentation in the *Collection* shows that Dodsley usually replaced Gray's capitalization of nouns with lower-case letters, and some place-name nouns with small capitals (Letter 125). Thus "Hours" (l. 1) became "hours," "Crowd" (l. 18) became "crowd," and "Attick" (l. 5) became "ATTIC." When these poems were reprinted in 1753 and 1768, however, each of these adjustments in the *Collection* was replaced by Gray's original manuscript reading.

Occasionally a capitalized noun was not changed in the *Collection*, as in "Contemplation's sober eye" ("Ode on the Spring," l. 31); but in the second and subsequent editions of the miscellany the normalization had its effect and the word became "contemplation's." Capitalization and punctuation in the 1753 and

1768 versions of both "Ode on the Spring" and "Ode on the Death of a Favourite Cat" are irregular, however: the *Collection* sometimes has a word capitalized that is lower-case in the 1753 and 1768 editions, but usually this situation is reversed. In the "Eton" ode, for instance, which Dodsley first published in folio in 1747, most nouns are capitalized and place-names are italicized. The capitals are dropped in the version in the *Collection*, and usually only the personifications are re-capitalized in the later editions. The italicized nouns, meanwhile — "*Henry's*" (l. 4), "*Windsor's*" (l. 6), "*Thames*" (l. 9) — are reduced to non-italicized small capitals in both the *Collection* and later editions. Finally, the stanzaic presentation of the "Ode on the Spring" in the *Collection* is unique. Gray ran the lines on in his manuscript; in the 1753 and 1768 editions the stanzas were separated but without any numbering; in the *Collection* the stanzas were separated and numbered by Roman numeral.

Dodsley's treatment of Collins's poems in the *Collection* is similar. In the "Ode, to a Lady" for instance — which Dodsley had first published in his *Museum* (1746), and which then appeared in revised form in the *Odes* (Millar, 1747) and the *Collection* (2nd edn., 1748) — the two printings that Dodsley supervised are alike in many ways, and at first glance one might conjecture that Dodsley used his *Museum* version as copy-text when he included the poem in the *Collection*. The details of punctuation are very similar, but in capitalization and italics the *Museum* version is actually much more closely followed by Millar's *Odes*. Italics disappear in the *Collection*, although small capitals often take their place; capitalization of nouns, including personifications, is generally eliminated. The stanzas are indicated by Roman numerals in both the *Museum* and *Collection* texts; in the *Odes* they are preceded by Arabics (a characteristic of that publication). It is obvious that at some points Dodsley drew upon the *Odes* version, though, for punctuation as well as for the text itself. The following example, however, demonstrates Dodsley's usual practice.

Museum (ll. 46-47):   Ev'n humble *H*——'s cottag'd Vale
                        Shall learn the sad-repeated Tale,

Odes (ll. 58-59):   Ev'n humble *Harting*'s cottag'd Vale
                        Shall learn the sad repeated Tale,

Collection (ll. 46-47):   Ev'n humble HARTING's cottage vale
                            Shall learn the sad-repeated tale,

Here we can see Dodsley following his earlier punctuation, modifying its italics and capitals, augmenting a substantive from the version printed in the *Odes* ("HARTING'S"), and (deliberately?) altering another ("cottage").

These examples from Gray and Collins point to a consistency of style throughout the six volumes of the *Collection*. Italics are removed except in titles and footnotes, and even there italics become less frequent in later editions. The italics, in turn, are often replaced by small capitals. Punctuation is normalized, and spelling often modernized. The stanzas are separated, usually by Roman numerals (this had been true of Dodsley's *Museum* as well). And capitalization, even in the case of some personifications, is usually abandoned. Dodsley's removal of capitals, is, of course, part of a larger trend in printing in the late 1740s;[23] but it is also one solution to the problem of reprinting together a large number of poems whose authors (and whose editors) have widely differing practices affecting accidentals. As "house style," Dodsley's imposition of his own taste in the *Collection* works well, but it will not serve for the modern editor who wishes to present his poet's own accidentals.

That this house style represented a solution to a particular problem is suggested by later editions of Gray's poetry. There, in the editions of 1753 and 1768, Gray's own stylistic preferences are restored. In the *Collection*, therefore, the text can usually be relied upon to represent an author's own work, or at least his compliance with his editor's revisions (unless external evidence proves otherwise); but the accidentals are certainly Dodsley's and his compositors'. If the scholarly editor's task is to choose a copy-text that approximates as closely as possible his author's own preferences in the presentation of accidentals, in this respect, then, he will have to approach Dodsley's *Collection of Poems* with caution, even as he learns to rely upon Dodsley's diligence as an editor and his zeal (for better or worse) for revised editions.

NOTES

1. In addition to the work of Chapman, Courtney, and Straus (cited below), see William B. Todd, "Concurrent Printing: An Analysis of Dodsley's *Collection of Poems by Several Hands*," *PBSA* 46 (1952): 45-57, and "Cancelled Readings in Dodsley's 'Collection of Poems,'" *NQ* 197 (1952): 143-144; and Donald D. Eddy, "Dodsley's *Collection of Poems by Several Hands* (Six Volumes), 1758: Index of Authors," *PBSA* 60 (1966): 9-30. I wish to thank Professor James E. Tierney for the opportunity to examine his edition of Dodsley's letters [now published], and for many helpful suggestions concerning this study.

2. James Boswell, *Life of Johnson*, ed. G. B. Hill, rev. L. F. Powell (1934), 1:326.

3. See R. D. Havens, "Changing Taste in the Eighteenth Century: A Study of Dryden's and Dodsley's Miscellanies," *PMLA* 44 (1929): 501-536.

4. "Dodsley's Collection of Poems by Several Hands," *Oxford Biblio-graphical Society: Proceedings & Papers* 3, pt. 3 (1933): 269.

5. *Dodsley's Collection of Poetry: Its Contents and Contributors* (1910), p. 2; this is corroborated by Dodsley's correspondence (BL Add. MS. 28959, ff. 10-11).

6. *Robert Dodsley: Poet, Publisher & Playwright* (1910), p. 102.

7. For a discussion of Dodsley's influence on Collins's texts, see the edition of Collins's works edited by Richard Wendorf and Charles Ryskamp (1979).

8. The information and quotations in this paragraph are taken from Straus, pp. 108-110; see also Ralph M. Williams, *Poet, Painter, and Parson: The Life of John Dyer* (1956), pp. 129, 136, 139.

9. *Correspondence of Thomas Gray*, ed. P. Toynbee and L. Whibley (1935), 1:294-295 (Letter 144). Further references to this edition are often provided by letter in the text.

10. Several other discrepancies should be noted. In one instance ("Harry," l. 35) the text in the *Collection* follows the Wharton text but was changed (presumably by the author) to "Susan" in later printings of the miscellany and in Dodsley's 1753 and 1768 editions of Gray's poetry (it appeared first as "Susan" in Gray's Commonplace Book). At another point ("beauteous," l. 14) Dodsley's reading differs from both Wharton and the 1753 and 1768 editions ("angel"); "beauteous" is also the reading in the Commonplace Book, however, and therefore it was apparently the reading in Gray's letter to Walpole as well (which Dodsley followed). Finally, in two places ("looks," l. 25; "tempts," l. 40), Dodsley's readings differ from both the Commonplace Book and Gray's letter to Wharton: "Eye" ("Eyes" in Wharton); "strikes." Here, however, Dodsley's readings were preserved in the editions of Gray's poetry published in 1753 and 1768, and thus it seems safe to conclude that Gray had originally suggested these readings in his letter to Walpole. Despite the recent editions of Gray's poetry by H. W. Starr and J. R. Hendrickson (1966) and Roger Lonsdale (1969), the problems of

textual transmission and determination of a copy-text for these poems appear not to have received a full textual discussion.

11. Letter 466, to James Beattie, who supervised the Foulis edition; see also Letter 465, to James Dodsley.

12. Letter 159. Gray also took Dodsley and his "matrons" to task for another variant, but he had in this case actually suggested the change and asked for Walpole's opinion (see Letters 157 and 159). Gray's attitude towards Dodsley in this series of letters suggests that Walpole himself was not responsible for the changes.

13. See Thomas Gray, *An Elegy Written in a Country Church Yard*, ed. F. G. Stokes (1929), pp. 19, 27, 34-35.

14. Letter 172; another letter to Dodsley (1:366) has not survived. For Gray's meetings with Dodsley, see Straus, pp. 158, 164.

15. *The Letters of William Shenstone*, ed. Marjorie Williams (1939), p. 131 (Letter LXIII). Further references to this edition are provided by letter in the text.

16. Cf. Shenstone's description of his friend at the head of Dodsley's collected correspondence: "A Person whose writings I esteem in common with the Publick; But of whose Simplicity, Benevolence, Humanity, & true Politeness, I have had repeated and particular experience" (BL Add. MS. 28959, f. 2).

17. *The Letters of Horace Walpole*, ed. Mrs. Paget Toynbee (1903), 3:195.

18. 8 October 1743 (Bodleian MS. Toynbee d. 19, ff. 5-6); *Honour* was published in December 1743.

19. 15 February 1758 (Bodleian MS. Eng. Letters d. 40, f. 113).

20. 7 July 1746 (Bodleian MS. Eng. Misc. d. 174, p. 15); cf. also pp. 71-72, regarding Cooper's *Letters Concerning Taste* (1754): "as I know you are so fond of accuracy, I have taken uncommon Pains & have polish'd these trifles as much as I was able." Thomas Lisle, who edited Edward Lisle's *Observations in Husbandry* (published by Dodsley in 1756), expressed similar confidence: "be so good as to correct what You find

amiss in them, & send them to the Press, without giving yourself the trouble of consulting me: I shall willingly stand to your amendments" (Bodleian MS. Eng. Letters d. 40, f. 107).

21. Dodsley altered both the accidentals and the substantives of early dramatic texts in compiling his *Select Collection of Old Plays* in 1744; see R. C. Bald, "Sir William Berkeley's *The Lost Lady*," *The Library* 4th ser., 17 (1937): 395-426, and A. T. Brissenden, "Dodsley's Copy-Text for *The Revenger's Tragedy* in his *Select Collection*," *The Library* 5th ser., 19 (1964): 254-258. Both Bald and Brissenden, drawing upon Dodsley's annotated copies of the texts, claim that he shared the role of normalizing accidentals with his compositors.

22. A similar case for alteration could be made for James Dodsley's handling of Gray's manuscripts (prepared for the printer) of "The Fatal Sisters," "The Descent of Odin," and "The Triumphs of Owen" when these pieces were included in *Poems by Mr. Gray* (1768). There is reason, of course, to believe that Gray "intended" his accidentals to follow the form Dodsley chose for them; this is his attitude, at least, towards the Foulis edition in 1768. Gray wrote to James Beattie: "please to observe, that I am entirely unversed in the doctrine of *Stops*, whoever therefore shall deign to correct them, will do me a friendly office: I wish I stood in need of no other correction" (Letter 466).

23. See Bertrand H. Bronson, *Printing as an Index of Taste in Eighteenth-Century England* (1958), reprinted in his *Facets of the Enlightenment* (1968), pp. 326-365. J. Smith, *The Printer's Grammar* (1755), indicates that authors themselves were sometimes given the choice of capitalization and italicization: "Before we actually begin to compose, we should be informed, either by the Author, or Master, after what manner our work is to be done; whether the old way, with Capitals to Substantives, and Italic to proper names; or after the more neat practice, all in Roman, and Capitals to Proper names, and Emphatical words" (p. 201); cited by Philip Gaskell, *A New Introduction to Bibliography* (1972), p. 339 n.

Chapter 9
The Secret Life of Type

PERHAPS YOU CAN remember, as I can, when only Frank Harris had a secret life — and told us about it. Now it seems as if everyone (and every *thing*) has a subterranean story to be told. Dogs have a secret life (if we stay up late enough to follow them). Dust has a secret life (if we have magnification enough to examine it). Bees, germs, plants, food, the brain, the unborn child, the Catholic Church: each has a hidden life, according to a tidal wave of confessional histories. Even Salvador Dalí's secret life is now in print, as if the artist who invited his guests to watch him masturbate ever had much to hide. Surely something as familiar and ubiquitous as typography must have a secret life as well. But where, exactly, shall we find it?

Not on the page you are currently reading — or at least not

Many academic writers hope to be able to engage a broad, general audience at some point in their careers, and it is with this larger readership in mind that I have written this introduction to the nature and history of typography. It attempts to do for Samuel Johnson's "common reader" what Paul Gutjahr and Megan Benton have done for an academic audience in their introduction to *Illuminating Letters: Typography and Literary Interpretation* (Amherst: Univ. of Massachusetts Press, 2001).

at first glance. The printed word is, by definition, the site of public rather than private discourse. Writers become authors once their work has been published, and something that is published belongs, by definition, in what Jürgen Habermas has called the public sphere. When readers encounter the printed word, moreover, the words they read are usually presented in a typographical format that is as neutral — as resolutely conventional — as possible. We are not supposed to notice the physical appearance of the letters themselves: they are supposed to be invisible, transparent; they are not supposed to draw attention to themselves. When they do, either the publisher is inept or the author is trying to tell you something that words alone cannot do.

Strong historical forces lie behind the conventionality — what we might call the carefully programmed banality — of most of the type specimens we encounter in our normal lives as readers. When moveable type was first created midway through the fifteenth century, all three major typographical families (roman, *italic*, and 𝔤𝔬𝔱𝔥𝔦𝔠) were derived from manuscript hands that flourished at the beginning of the incunabular period (literally the "cradle" or "infancy" of printing). Capital roman letters had their origin in the square capitals found in Latin inscriptions on classical columns and buildings; Trajan's column, near the Roman Forum, is the most revered example. Because these capital letters were less amenable to the needs of everyday writing, a form of cursive ("running") script, with rounded Roman capitals, evolved during the early centuries of the modern era. Smaller letters, also derived from classical Roman capitals, appeared just as the empire fell, and these were then codified during the medieval period into what has become known as the Carolingian minuscule (capitals, on the other hand, are known as majuscules). Further refinement of these letterforms by Renaissance humanists eventually produced a prototype for the earliest printing in roman, which seems to have appeared in 1467, over a decade later than the publication of Gutenberg's famous 42-line Bible.

Gutenberg's Bible — and indeed every text issued during the first ten years or so of the incunabular period — was printed in what we today call gothic typeface, although at various times it has also been called "English," "textura," or simply "black letter." It is important for us to remember that the first books printed in England also appeared in black letter, that the first English book completely printed in roman type did not appear until 1555 (almost 90 years later than on the continent), that the authorized King James version of the Bible was printed in black letter in 1611, and that royal proclamations were printed in this style until 1730. By the mid-seventeenth century, however, gothic type was already viewed by English printers as being out of date, and the last English Bible printed in black letter appeared in 1640. Gothic lettering continued to survive pre-cisely where it still flourishes today, on the mastheads of English and American newspapers. And in Germany, of course, they continue to order these matters differently, retaining not only their predilection for gothic script, but also their use of the long "s" (with all of its ligatures) and the Capitalization of common Nouns — both of which were long ago discarded by French and English printers, as we shall see.

As its name suggests, the third general family of Western typefaces, italic, is derived from Italian sources, particularly the chancery hands that proliferated during the Italian Renais-sance. The Venetian printer, publisher, and scholar Aldo Manu-tio (commonly known today as Aldus Manutius) introduced a cursive Latin script for learned books in 1501 and then adopted it for his celebrated books in smaller formats (our earliest pocket-books, so to speak). Italian printers employed their own versions of the Aldine italic for texts printed in either Latin or the vernacular throughout the sixteenth century, thereby rounding off my argument concerning the historically based conventionality of type. When these three typefaces were first introduced, their basic shapes were already familiar to the small audiences capable of reading Renaissance manuscripts and — by extension — early printed texts. Our first printers shrewdly decided to emphasize continuity rather than innovation in the physical appearance of their letters. Their technology was revolutionary, but their product was not; and it is therefore not surprising that many readers found the first generation of printed books to be less attractive than their calligraphic counterparts, nor that some collectors actually prided themselves on only purchasing (or commissioning) books in manuscript form. This moment of cultural differentiation should not be lost on us today, given the continuing devotion to print culture within the opening decades of what is called both "the electronic age" and "the late age of print."

The letterforms we encounter today therefore have a long history (over two thousand years, in the case of roman), and it is a history of slow evolution rather than abrupt cultural or visual change. Each of the three families of typographical lettering adopted conventional features from a local calligraphic tradition, and each scribal family in turn generated its own conventions — in capitalization, punctuation, and the use of ligatures, for example — as each typeface became something of a visual universe unto itself, separated from and uncontaminated by competing typographical forms.

But then something interesting happened. Italic type found its way into German printing by 1520 or so, into French books by 1530, and into English texts by 1555, but often with a difference, for the typeface that had originally been created by Aldus as an *alternative* to roman or gothic was also being used piecemeal within roman texts, in marginal notes, or for decorative purposes on title-pages. An early English edition of Horace, for example, might well be printed in italic with roman notes, but this would pose an exception. The normal practice was for books to be printed in roman with insertions and supplements in italic (as in an italic dedication, preface, or introduction to a roman text). The seventeenth-century Swiss grammarian Guy Miege was quite clear on this point: "In the way of Printing, the *Roman* Letter is the chief and predominant; the *Italick* being only used for Distinctions sake, but chiefly for Proper Names, Quotations, and Change of Language" — an explanation made all the more telling by appropriately (and ironically) placing the word "*Roman*" in italic. At work in these "Distinctions," moreover, are hierarchical, nationalistic, aesthetic, and even gender issues that begin to suggest the secret life of type.

What happens, for instance, when two families of typeface are mixed together? In English and American printing, it is still normal for the roman letter to predominate and thus to determine the conventions of the text in hand. We no longer italicize proper names and quotations, but we do italicize foreign words, dedications, stage directions, some running heads, some subtitles, some prefaces, and even the occasional *distinctive* word. Italic sets apart certain words or certain elements in a publication and thereby produces what Johanna Drucker has called the "marked" text. Drucker, who is both a critic and an artist of the book, has a special interest in typographical features that manipulate how a given text is read and interpreted: the choice and size of type, the juxtaposition of types and type sizes, the use of boldface and color — all of the elements that we normally associate with commercial or bureaucratic texts that attempt to provoke a particular form of behavior in the reader (buy this; don't do that).

Against this aggressive form of printing Drucker juxtaposes the unmarked text, "the even gray page of prose and poetic convention" whose typography is seemingly invisible, its text neutral and natural to the reader (the text you're reading, in other words). This is a helpful distinction, but finer distinctions may be even more useful. It has been pointed out, for instance, that no printed text is really unmarked. "Once given visual form," Megan Benton and Paul Gutjahr have argued, texts are "implicitly coded" in ways that signal, however subtly, their nature and purpose as well as how their creators wish them to be approached and valued. Designers and printers (good designers and printers) constantly make decisions about which typeface is most appropriate for a given text or genre of printing; one of them, the Canadian poet and typographer Robert Bringhurst, has gone so far as to claim that typography is "an essential act of interpretation, full of endless opportunities for insight or obtuseness."

I'll return to the thorny issue of interpretation at the close of this essay. What is not in dispute, I think, is the fact that for *readers* (although perhaps not always for writers) linguistic texts don't exist apart from their manner of presentation, whether they be printed, handwritten, illuminated, engraved, abbreviated, digitized, or otherwise manipulated into forms that remain accessible to us. Linguistic texts are conventionally published (and thereby enter the public sphere) by means of a series of typographical marks. Thus there is no such thing as an unmarked text, even when there is only one choice of typographical presentation; it is, after all, a choice — or, if not a conscious choice, at least an accepted form of presentation that differs from a myriad of other possible presentational forms. This essay, for instance, appears in the style (Minion) of the larger book in which it is printed. Had the designer and I decided to print this chapter in a different typeface (gothic, italic, or an antique roman such as Granjon; or perhaps a blunt, pared-down *sans serif* version of what you now see), you — as readers — would immediately begin to judge the significance (or appropriateness) of this visual aberration. We have chosen, instead, to employ a handsome and accessible font that I also selected for my previous book, *Sir Joshua Reynolds*, and which we use at the Boston Athenæum for our annual reports and occasional papers. Minion, in short, has been carefully chosen, along with all of the other "bibliographical codes" that determine the relative attractiveness and *lisibilité* of the printed page.

To mix typographical elements within the same text might be thought of as a secondary (and often more noticeably visible and dramatic) form of marking, of making distinctions. Most texts, including this one, are hybrid forms, employing both roman and italic typefaces, and the hybrid nature of such texts often produces an interesting paradox involving the issue of hierarchy. Roman is usually the "chief and predominant" family of type within modern Western texts; italic is the alternative typeface, playing a subordinate role and often marking what is less important or less central in the text. But when italic is used for emphasis or distinction, as it still is today, it actually supercedes and thereby trumps the predominant typographical form. Sometimes *less* is more.

This distinction was not lost on eighteenth-century printers and grammarians, many of whom worried about typographical decorum in terms which make it clear that much more than the politics of typographical power was actually at stake. Many writers warned against the indiscriminate mixing of forms, but no one more vehemently than Philip Luckombe, who in a history of printing published in 1770 praised "noble" and "bold" roman typefaces, described the "soft and tender" faces of italic letters, and argued that letters of "an erect position" should not be "promiscuously" joined with those of "an oblique inclination." At play here are both gender and sexual differentiation, issues that re-emerged in Victorian England when the typefaces that superceded eighteenth-century Caslon were criticized for refining masculine forms into effeminate shapes. But even in the eighteenth century there was an increasing interest among English printers in the comparative simplicity and elegance of continental forms, especially those created by French designers. It was out of this artistic ferment that John Baskerville and John Bell began to make their contributions to English printing during the second half of the century.

If I placed two small books in your hands, both published in 1700, one in Paris, the other in London, the remarkable difference between English printing and its counterpart on the continent would immediately be apparent to you (figures 15-16). The format, binding, and paper of the two books might look similar, but a careful perusal of almost any page of text in each volume would quickly disclose what I'm going to call the comparative *modernity* of presentation in the French book. The Parisian text will almost certainly appear to be less cluttered: it will contain more generous margins and more spacing between lines (and perhaps between letters and words as well), thereby producing a shorter and more open textblock that has become more inviting to the reader. The letters themselves will be thinner and perhaps more attenuated, and if there are larger visual elements at play (a vignette or printer's device, for example) they will be more delicately designed as well. You will also be struck by the comparative lack of typographical diversity on the French page. Instead of the characteristic English mishmash of competing typeforms and type sizes, you will encounter a more consistently printed text with fewer excursions into italic, a more sparing use of capitalization, and a less frequent employment of small caps (some-

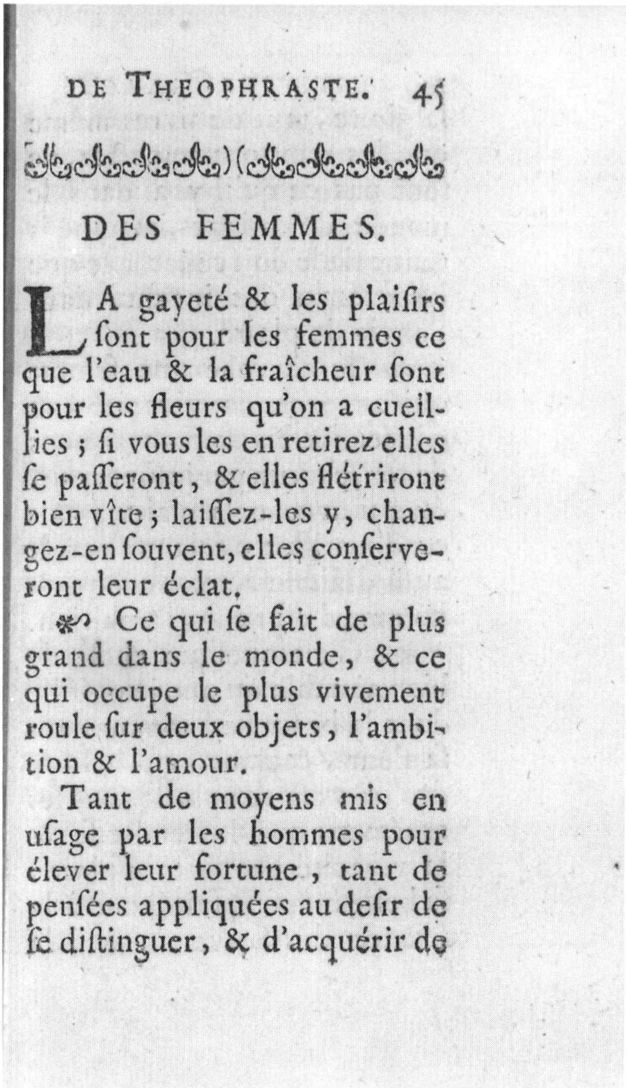

DE THEOPHRASTE. 45

DES FEMMES.

L A gayeté & les plaifirs font pour les femmes ce que l'eau & la fraîcheur font pour les fleurs qu'on a cueillies ; fi vous les en retirez elles fe pafferont, & elles flétriront bien vîte ; laiffez-les y, changez-en fouvent, elles conferveront leur éclat.

Ce qui fe fait de plus grand dans le monde, & ce qui occupe le plus vivement roule fur deux objets, l'ambition & l'amour.

Tant de moyens mis en ufage par les hommes pour élever leur fortune, tant de penfées appliquées au defir de fe diftinguer, & d'acquérir de

FIGURE 15.
Alleaume (attributed author), *Suite des Caracteres de Theophraste* (Paris: Estienne Michallet, 1700). By permission of The Houghton Library, Harvard College Library.

MEMOIRS, &c.   91

ment: For it was he chiefly that broke off that *Match*, when he saw how much King *James* suffer'd in his Honour, through the manner he was treated in it, which he found out sooner than the King did himself. It's none of the least Proofs of the Duke of *Buckingham*'s Innocency in these matters, that *Spanhemius* in his History of the *Electrice Palatine*, (writ long after *Buckingham*'s Death) speaks always honourably of him in the Business of the *Palatinate*; whereas at the same time he exposes King *James*'s Conduct.

It's a vulgar mistake, that he came to be the *First Minister*, merely through the Caprice of King *James*; for the Court unanimously promoted his Interest, and recommended him to the highest Favour, in opposition to *Somerset*, whose Arrogancy, Covetousness, and Pride, had disoblig'd every body, and made both the King and the Court weary of him. No Servant did his Master more Honour in *the Magnificence of his Train, and the splendid Manner of his living*; especially in his *Embassy* to *France*; where in the Gracefulness of his Person, and Noblenefs of his Behaviour and Equipage, he outdid any thing that ever was
seen

FIGURE 16.
James Welwood, *Memoirs of the Most Material Transactions in England* (London: Timothy Goodwin, 1700). By permission of the Boston Athenæum.

times called CAPS and SMALL CAPS). In short, the French page will be less crowded and more homogenous; its words will not be found clamoring for attention, possibly at each other's expense. You will find it — dare I invoke the word? — not only more refined, but also more completely *rationalized*.

We need to ask ourselves, however, whether there might not be some essential logic at work within the more variegated English texts at the turn of the eighteenth century. Is it possible that the English propensity for italic, capitals, and small caps was based on a practical schema concerning hierarchy and subordination? Had the French, by 1700, abandoned an important typographical form of differentiation? In theory, at least, the English printers and grammarians knew what they were doing. Italic, as we have seen, was to be used for proper names, quotations, and words in a foreign language. Capitalization was to be employed for words beginning a sentence or a line of poetry, for proper nouns, and for what were called "emphatical" words (usually "substantives," what we today call common nouns, although other words, especially pronouns and adjectives, could also have particular emphasis placed upon them).

In practice, however, English printers produced thousands and thousands of books containing an extraordinary hodgepodge of typographical elements. Most texts printed in the second half of the seventeenth century and the opening decades of the eighteenth capitalized virtually every noun, common as well as proper. Because proper names and other substantives could be either capitalized or italicized (or both!), and because the English relished the use of small caps for emphasis as well, we often discover a remarkable clogging of the typographical arteries. An emphatic word could appear, for example, as "liberty," "Liberty," "*liberty*," "*Liberty*," "LIBERTY," or "LIBERTY" — and it often did. Some of this visual variety could be harnessed to mark important distinctions within a given text, especially in theological discourses with their fine hierarchical gradations. But in most of these books there is little coherence or logic whatsoever. What the English preached at the turn of the century, particularly the occasional use of capitalization to mark important common nouns, their counterparts in Rome and Madrid faithfully practiced and their counterparts in Paris and Frankfurt happily abjured — the French essentially abandoning the capital while the Germans carefully husbanded it.

And then, beginning in the 1740s, books produced in London began to resemble their Parisian *frères et sœurs*. The capitalization of common nouns began to disappear; italics were more or less restricted to foreign words, place names, and quotations; and small caps began to take their modern position at the opening of paragraphs and in various stage directions. There are exceptions, of course, but by 1770 it was more likely that an English book was printed in what I call the new style rather than in the old. By the 1790s, moreover, we begin to encounter what is essentially the modern English page: the fussiness of excessive capitals, small caps, and italics has disappeared; the long "s" and its ligatures have been abandoned (beginning with John Bell's edition of Shakespeare in 1785, to be precise); and more leading (and thus more space) has been introduced into the design of each *mise-en-page*. I could in fact show you a late-eighteenth-century copy of an English play (figure 17) that you could not distinguish from the handsome edition of George Bernard Shaw published by the Bodley Head in 1970.

Why should such basic changes in typographical convention have taken place in the middle decades of the eighteenth century? Or, to put the question more pointedly, why didn't these developments occur earlier, as they had in France? English Bibles and books of common prayer, after all, had been printed

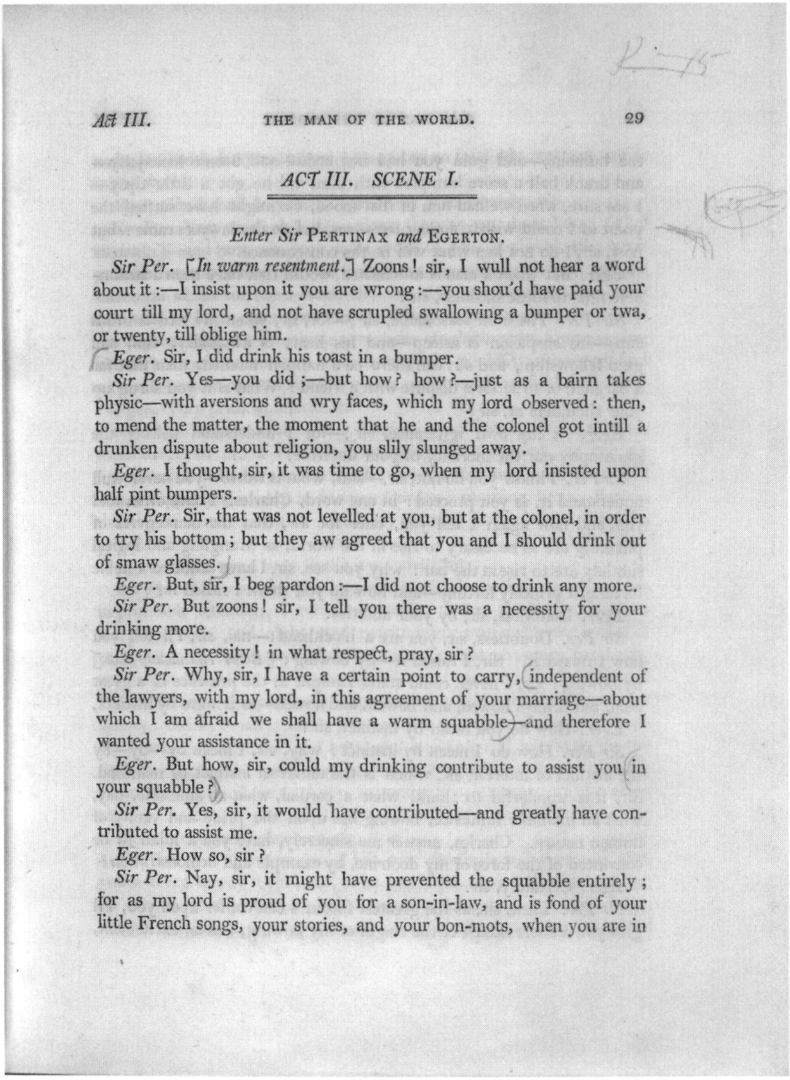

ACT III. SCENE I.

Enter Sir PERTINAX *and* EGERTON.

Sir Per. [*In warm resentment.*] Zoons! sir, I wull not hear a word about it :—I insist upon it you are wrong :—you shou'd have paid your court till my lord, and not have scrupled swallowing a bumper or twa, or twenty, till oblige him.

Eger. Sir, I did drink his toast in a bumper.

Sir Per. Yes—you did ;—but how? how?—just as a bairn takes physic—with aversions and wry faces, which my lord observed : then, to mend the matter, the moment that he and the colonel got intill a drunken dispute about religion, you slily slunged away.

Eger. I thought, sir, it was time to go, when my lord insisted upon half pint bumpers.

Sir Per. Sir, that was not levelled at you, but at the colonel, in order to try his bottom ; but they aw agreed that you and I should drink out of smaw glasses.

Eger. But, sir, I beg pardon :—I did not choose to drink any more.

Sir Per. But zoons! sir, I tell you there was a necessity for your drinking more.

Eger. A necessity! in what respect, pray, sir ?

Sir Per. Why, sir, I have a certain point to carry, independent of the lawyers, with my lord, in this agreement of your marriage—about which I am afraid we shall have a warm squabble—and therefore I wanted your assistance in it.

Eger. But how, sir, could my drinking contribute to assist you in your squabble ?

Sir Per. Yes, sir, it would have contributed—and greatly have contributed to assist me.

Eger. How so, sir ?

Sir Per. Nay, sir, it might have prevented the squabble entirely ; for as my lord is proud of you for a son-in-law, and is fond of your little French songs, your stories, and your bon-mots, when you are in

FIGURE 17.
Charles Macklin, *The Man of the World*
(London: John Bell, 1793).
By permission of The Huntington.

in the new style throughout the seventeenth and early eighteenth centuries, and no books were more important, or more
frequently consulted, than these two volumes. These changes,
on the other hand, took place within a linguistic environment
that was still partially in flux. As late as 1721, for example, Isaac
Watts could write in his *Art of Reading and Writing English* that
he follows the "old and usual Custom" of listing twenty-four letters in the alphabet, although he wishes that "our Fathers" had
made "v" and "j" consonants "and called them *ja* and *vee*, and
thus made Six-and-twenty." Most of his contemporaries *did*
make twenty-six, but even as "j" and "v" entered the hornbook
and the printing house there were continuing debates about
how the various letters should be pronounced ("ja" is not our
"jay," after all) and whether "h" was a proper letter in English or
merely a mark of aspiration.

Benjamin Franklin, who began life as a printer (or more precisely as his brother's printer's devil), pointed out, moreover,
that there were two practical reasons for retaining the capitalization of common nouns.* Because so many books were still
read out loud, Franklin argued that capitalization helped the
speaker judge which words deserved particular emphasis: "the
Eye generally slides forward three or four Words before the
Voice" and we therefore rely upon distinctions within the visual
field in order to modulate our expression. But Franklin was also
concerned about the difficulties foreigners would encounter as
they attempted to decipher what was essentially a less mediated
text. Capitalization was particularly helpful to those who were
not well acquainted with English and its "prodigious Number"
of words that are both verbs and substantives — a phenomenon
that is much rarer in French. Franklin (and who would know

---

* The following three paragraphs are taken from Chapter 10, where these
issues are discussed at greater length.

better?) ascribed this change to "the Fancy of Printers," who believed that the suppression of capitals "shows the Character to greater Advantage; those Letters prominent above the line disturbing its even regular Appearance." The "Effect of this Change is so considerable," Franklin wrote, that a learned Frenchman who used to read English books with some ease now found them difficult to understand, blaming the stylistic obscurity of modern English writers because he did not realize that the printing conventions themselves had changed. Franklin called these changes "Improvements *backwards*," but by the time he voiced these concerns in the 1770s and 1780s, he was clearly the odd man out.

So, in effect, was Samuel Johnson when he noted that "Our language, for almost a century, has, by the concurrence of many causes, been gradually departing from its original *Teutonick* character, and deviating towards a *Gallick* structure and phraseology, from which it ought to be our endeavour to recal it." By 1755, when Johnson published these words in the "Preface" to his great *Dictionary* (in the new style), the typographical floodgates had stood open for almost twenty years. Johnson's own work as a lexicographer was, if not directly responsible for supporting these changes, at least consistent with them, for he found himself contending with a language that was "a confused heap of words, without dependence, and without relation." Johnson's extraordinary achievement was to impose order on what he called "the boundless chaos of a living speech." He did so by establishing principles of selection, purity, and authority, thereby reducing "to method" a language that was "energetick without rules." It was, famously, a solitary task completed by a single scholar in the space of seven years, whereas it had taken the forty French academicians forty years to complete their own *dictionnaire*.

In terms of the wider culture surrounding him, however, Johnson was far from alone. An act of Parliament in 1752 finally led to the adoption of the Gregorian calendar, thus placing England temporally in step with the rest of Western Europe. While the new calendar was being fiercely debated in the pages of the *Gentleman's Magazine*, there were similar discussions of whether the English should rationalize their weights, their measures, and their coinage, and whether a national census should be introduced (it was not). This, it seems to me, is precisely the cultural climate in which printing conventions could also undergo a similar transformation from the old style to the new. Despite the Jacobite rising in 1745, the Seven Years' War that began in 1756, and a Hanoverian dynasty on the throne, the English were nonetheless willing to synchronize themselves in their calendars and on the printed page roughly at mid-century, at high Georgian noon.

I have focused on the standardization of printing conventions in England during the eighteenth century for a number of important reasons. First, because distinctions between upper- and lower-case letters, or between roman and italic fonts, are relatively easy to parse. Second, because capitalization and italicization immediately raise issues of hierarchy, nationality, gender, and (as we have seen) even sexual decorum. (In most Western texts, for example, italic is the exotic "other": marginalized, colonized, and yet — as I have shown — capable of usurping power within the roman republic of letters.) And finally, because we can show how the English standardization of its printing conventions unfolded within a broader cultural climate in which our predecessors were willing to question traditional forms and to entertain quite different alternatives.

The American printer Daniel Berkeley Updike once remarked that "we unconsciously govern our printing by the kind of life we approve." A Marxist would phrase this rather differently, emphasizing ideology — internalized to the point where it becomes invisible — as the shaping factor in cultural production, but the point is essentially the same: typography, like any other human artifact, bears the impress of the culture that produces it. For American and English readers, the eighteenth century remains a critical period in the history of typography because of the gradual but decisive changes that produced the modern, standardized page of text with which we are so familiar. The codification of printing conventions both reflects and participates in the larger cultural forces that England entertained — and in many ways embraced — halfway through the century.

This is not to say, however, that typography actually performs an interpretative act, as Robert Bringhurst has argued in *The Elements of Typographical Style*. His full argument is worth quoting. "Typography is to literature as musical performance is to composition: an essential act of interpretation, full of endless opportunities for insight or obtuseness." The analogy is interesting, but faulty. Composers compose music (in their heads, at their pianos) and then give that music material form through a series of marks (musical notations) that are later printed on pieces of paper. Conductors and musicians perform a composer's music by reading (and interpreting) the musical score; and each performance therefore is, indeed, an essential act of interpretation, full of opportunities for insight or obtuseness. Authors write literary works (in their heads, at their workstations) and then give those works material form through a series of marks that are written and later printed on pieces of paper. Readers (Samuel Johnson's common readers as well as professional literary critics) interpret a writer's work by reading the printed text; each reading is an interpretive performance, whether it be silent or spoken, private or public, internalized or given verbal form.

Although one can easily cite exceptions to this rule, typography is normally not itself interpretive or performative; this is what we as readers do. But typography is arguably the most important element in the creation of the material text, and the decisions that authors, printers, and publishers make about the presentation of a given text often influence the process of interpretation. Like the many other elements of a bibliographical code, typography may present itself as conventionally — as neutrally, as blandly — as possible. Or it may, as Bringhurst nicely phrases it, aspire to "a kind of statuesque transparency," drawing attention to the text but also relinquishing the attention it has drawn to itself as a part of that text. In the seventeenth and eighteenth centuries, for example, capitalized and italicized personifications ("While *Spring* shall pour his Show'rs, as oft he wont, / And bathe thy breathing Tresses, meekest *Eve*") reminded readers that these figures were intended to be visualized, often as classical deities with their full panoply of allegorical attributes. Or typography may be palpably aggressive, an end in itself, as Jerome McGann has remarked of William Morris's typographical excesses at the Kelmscott Press: "The work forces us to attend to its immediate and iconic condition, as if the words were images or objects themselves, as if they were *values* in themselves (rather than vehicles for delivering some further value or meaning)."

Trying to *read* the Kelmscott Chaucer is hard work indeed, and not just because Morris's typography is so very different from what we're accustomed to (figure 18). Each opening is an elaborate diptych in which type, headpiece, initial letters, illustrations, and framing devices work in concert to produce a hybrid form of text and image. The linguistic text survives, of

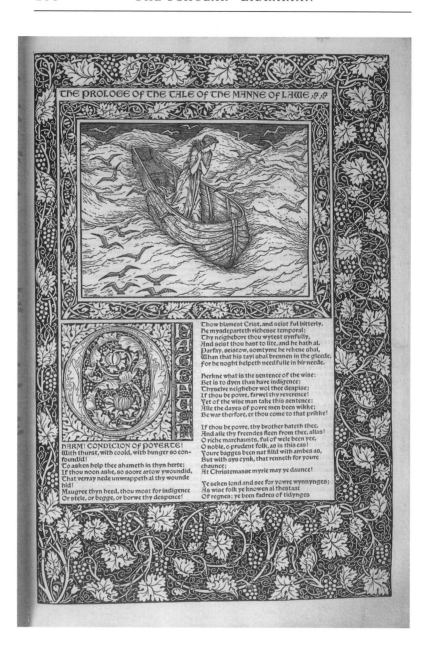

FIGURE 18.
Geoffrey Chaucer, *The Works of Geoffrey Chaucer*
(Hammersmith: Kelmscott Press, 1896).
By permission of the Boston Athenæum.

course, but it is overpowered by all of the elements — including the almost calligraphic black-letter typeface — that both define and surround it. We might generously think of Morris's project as an interartistic interpretation of the medieval world in which Chaucer lived, but we are more likely to interpret it as an embodiment of the "Pre-Raphaelite" values to which Morris and his contemporaries were so fiercely devoted.

Morris knew, as we should, that type has a history. His creation of a new typeface for his Kelmscott Chaucer was obviously influenced by the gothic letters printed in early-modern England as well as in Frankfurt and Mainz. Morris also knew, as we now should, that typography is fully implicated in the culture in which it is created and used, and that the elements at play within a page of text therefore perform complex (and sometimes conflicting) roles. He also knew that Chaucer's text, like any text, does not exist (for readers at least) apart from its material form, and that typography is therefore a crucial element in the creation, interpretation, and transmission of the material text. We may experience type as a transparent medium, but it is anything but invisible. It is, in fact, the word made visible — the word made public — and thereby open to those acts of interrogation upon which the vibrancy of a culture depends.

Chapter 10

Abandoning the Capital in Eighteenth-Century London

Total and sudden transformations
of a language seldom happen.

Samuel Johnson

T HIS ESSAY attempts to define a problem concerning
printing history and cultural change that has intrigued
and often baffled me for the past twenty-five years. I
begin by describing a phenomenon that is literally minuscule:
the gradual abandonment of pervasive capital letters (majuscules), as well as italics, in English books published during the
middle decades of the eighteenth century. I attempt to relate
this important change in printing practice to the roles of
author, bookseller, and printer during this period, to the growth
(and diversification) of the reading public in England, and to

This is the "seedling" essay for the broadly conceived book on printing conventions in eighteenth-century London on which I am currently engaged.
This chapter first appeared in *Reading, Society and Politics in Early Modern
England*, edited by Kevin Sharpe and Steven N. Zwicker (Cambridge: Cambridge Univ. Press, 2003), pp. 72-98.

other cultural phenomena of the 1750s — the publication of Johnson's *Dictionary* and the adoption of the Gregorian calendar, in particular — with which these changes in the printing house might profitably be associated. My research suggests that such a fundamental shift in printing conventions was closely tied to a pervasive interest in refinement, regularity, and even cultural conformity at mid-century. But such a change also reveals the conflicting emotions English men and women of the eighteenth century continued to harbor concerning their country's relationship to the rest of Europe. Samuel Johnson noted that "Our language, for almost a century, has, by the concurrence of many causes, been gradually departing from its original *Teutonick* character, and deviating towards a *Gallick* structure and phraseology, from which it ought to be our endeavour to recal it."[1] But by 1755, when Johnson published these words — in the new style — in the "Preface" to his *Dictionary*, the typographical floodgates had stood open for almost twenty years.

I

My first confrontation with what I now realize was a sweeping transformation in the appearance and "readability" of the printed page in eighteenth-century England occurred when Charles Ryskamp and I began preparing our edition of the poetry of William Collins in the mid-1970s. Collins enjoyed an unusual career as a writer, publishing a number of poems while he was still at Winchester and Oxford, orchestrating a somewhat successful assault on London in his early twenties, and then essentially disappearing from the literary scene in 1747, at the age of twenty-five. In deciding which version of Collins's *Persian Eclogues* of 1742 to accept as copy-text for our critical edition, we discovered that the revised edition of 1757 (entitled *Oriental Eclogues*) contained not only substantive variants but a host of changes in its "accidentals" as well: nouns other than proper names were no longer capitalized, and many of the words and phrases in italic were stripped of their distinctive styling. The difference between the presentation of the accidentals in these two editions can be gauged in the opening two lines of the poem (figures 19-20):

> 1742: Ye *Persian* Maids, attend your Poet's Lays,
>   And hear how Shepherds pass their golden Days:

> 1757: Ye Persian maids, attend your poet's lays,
>   And hear how shepherds pass their golden days.

Our attempt to account for the changes to be found in the second edition was doubly difficult. We discovered, in the first place, that Collins's modern editors had rejected the later edition's substantive alterations — usually defined as the verbal changes that affect the meaning of the text — because Collins was thought to be insane (and therefore incapable of revising his own poetry) in the 1750s. After looking closely at the surviving evidence, however, I concluded that the poet, despite the vaguely defined illness from which he suffered, was "able and eager to perform additional revision as late as 1756,"[2] and we therefore accepted, for the first time in the long trail of modern textual transmission, the substantive variants as they appeared in the text of the *Oriental Eclogues.*

It proved just as difficult, however, to determine a proper copy-text for a poem that had undergone such significant transformation in the space of only fifteen years. Under normal circumstances, a work with this kind of printing history would have prompted a straightforward editorial decision in the 1970s to follow the first edition as copy-text because that text would be most likely to preserve the author's intentions regarding accidentals (spelling, punctuation, and other elements of the formal presentation of the text). The edition would then incorporate authorial revisions from the later printing into the base text, and these revisions would be modified, if necessary, to conform to the presentation of the copy-text. These are the procedures laid down by W. W. Greg in his classic essay on "The Rationale of Copy-Text" and subsequently refined and codified by Fredson Bowers and other textual editors and theorists.[3]

But the *Persian* and *Oriental Eclogues* pose a special problem in the modification of accidentals, standing as they do on opposite sides of what Bertrand Bronson has called the "Great Divide" in eighteenth-century printing practice. In his essay on "Printing as an Index of Taste," Bronson was the first modern scholar, I believe, to point out that what I have described in the transmission of Collins's text was actually characteristic of printing practices in London from roughly 1745 to 1755: the highly mannered look of the typical English page of the preceding century had rather suddenly become (to impose *my* terms) the less emphatic, less cluttered, and less distinctive page that we expect to encounter in books published today. Bronson was aware, of course, that inconsistencies existed within the printing of a single author's works during the first half of the century, and he conceded, in a footnote, that books in a smaller format were more likely to retain their vigorous capitalization. But it was nevertheless clear to him "that there is a quite abrupt shift of convention just at the midpoint of the century. Before 1750 poetry was likely to be generously capitalized; after 1750 it was likely to be given a modern capitalization. There are exceptions on either side of the line, but they

(5)

ECLOGUE the FIRST.

SELIM; *or, the Shepherd's Moral.*

SCENE, *a Valley near* Bagdat.

TIME, *the* MORNING.

Y E *Perſian* Maids, attend your Poet's Lays,
    And hear how Shepherds paſs their golden
        Days:
Not all are bleſt, whom Fortune's Hand ſuſtains
With Wealth in Courts, nor all that haunt the Plains:
Well may your Hearts believe the Truths I tell,
'Tis Virtue makes the Bliſs, where'er we dwell.

Thus *Selim* ſung ; by ſacred Truth inſpir'd;
No Praiſe the Youth, but her's alone deſir'd:
Wiſe in himſelf, his meaning Songs convey'd
Informing Morals to the Shepherd Maid,

B   Or

FIGURE 19.
William Collins, *Persian Eclogues,* (1742).
By permission of The Houghton Library, Harvard College Library.

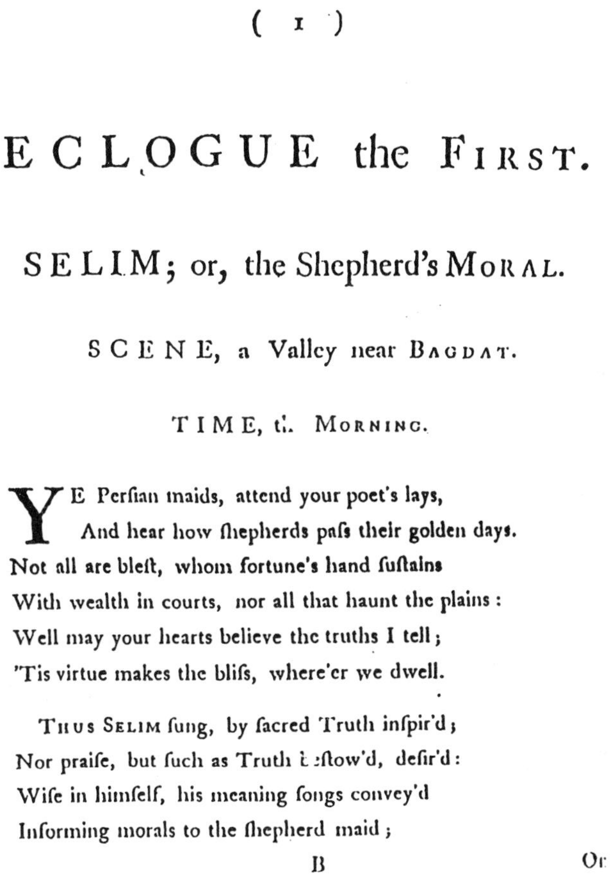

(1)

E C L O G U E the F I R S T.

S E L I M; or, the Shepherd's M O R A L.

S C E N E, a Valley near B A G D A T.

T I M E, t.'. M O R N I N G.

Y E Perſian maids, attend your poet's lays,
And hear how ſhepherds paſs their golden days.
Not all are bleſt, whom fortune's hand ſuſtains
With wealth in courts, nor all that haunt the plains :
Well may your hearts believe the truths I tell ;
'Tis virtue makes the bliſs, where'er we dwell.

THUS SELIM ſung, by ſacred Truth inſpir'd ;
Nor praiſe, but ſuch as Truth ſʒſlow'd, deſir'd :
Wiſe in himſelf, his meaning ſongs convey'd
Informing morals to the ſhepherd maid ;

B   Or

FIGURE 20.
William Collins, *Oriental Eclogues*, (1757).
By permission of The Houghton Library, Harvard College Library.

do not conceal the fact that 1750 is the Great Divide." And prose, he adds, "seems to have followed roughly the same course."[4] Given the inherent conservatism of printing as a trade, the phenomenon Bronson first described took place virtually overnight, transforming "the whole visual effect of a page of type" and consequently demanding a "change in psychological response" in us, as readers.[5]

In the case of a poet such as Collins, with his heavy investment in allegorical personification, we immediately sense a radical difference in the visual texture of his poetry as well as the dilemma of distinguishing between what is figurative and what is literal in his verse. The decision that Charles Ryskamp and I faced almost twenty-five years ago was therefore a difficult one indeed. If we chose the later text as our copy, we would both be imposing a form of Greg's "tyranny of the copy-text" by allowing the choice of substantives to rule the accidentals *and* ignoring the careful distinctions established within the printing houses of the early 1740s, when Collins was most active as a publishing poet. If, on the other hand, we returned to the presentation of accidentals in the 1742 edition, we would not be able to suggest — at least not in the text of the poem itself — the major departures in stylistic presentation occurring within the author's own lifetime. We finally decided to retain the accidentals of the *Persian Eclogues* in our eclectic, "amalgamated" text, and to address the editorial dilemma itself at length in the textual commentary. But this fundamental change in printing practice has continued to haunt me. Why did such a radical transformation take place? Who was responsible for it? How, precisely, did it unfold? And why did such an all-encompassing change occur at this particular moment, roughly at the midpoint of the eighteenth century?

I I

We know that writers and printers had already experimented with the stylistic presentation of their works for at least two hundred years. In the unpublished final chapter of his Lyell Lectures devoted to Pope and the eighteenth-century book trade, David Foxon noted that Ben Jonson abandoned the free use of capitals in preparing his folio *Workes* for publication in 1616. Jonson reserved final polishing for the fine-paper folio copies of his play *Every Man out of his Humour* while also taking a further step towards what Foxon calls "the classical tradition" by printing the names of the characters in his plays in caps and small caps — not just in the scene headings and speech prefixes, but in the text itself.[6] John Ogilby, on the other hand, adopted a typographical style later in the century that was abundantly capitalized, and Abraham Cowley invested equally heavily in italics.[7] Perhaps the most systematic of authors, moreover, was Edward Benlowes, whose *Theophila* of 1652 capitalizes every noun (as well as every pronoun relating to God, angels, or the soul), generously italicizes words for emphasis, and for even greater stress prints some words in capitals and small caps, with the deity always printed in full capitals.[8] The result, of course, is a textual page filled with the intricacies of hierarchical differentiation.

We discover a similar concern with "the visual language of typography" in what D. F. McKenzie has characterized as "a new and intimate form of teamwork between author or editor, bookseller and printer" at the turn of the eighteenth century.[9] In revising and reprinting his Restoration plays for a new, collected edition in 1710, William Congreve collaborated with the publisher Jacob Tonson and the printer John Watts to produce classicized texts that attempt to bridge "the gap between the fleeting image on a stage and the printed words on a page."[10] Congreve and Tonson did so by carefully choosing capitals and small caps for headlines and character groupings and by introducing headpieces and other printers' devices to separate act from act and scene from scene — an innovation that enunciated the scenic design of the plays for the first time in print and thereby repudiated the normal presentation of dramatic texts throughout the seventeenth century. In his plays as well as in his novel *Incognita*, McKenzie argues, Congreve was intent on making reading "a dramatic experience."[11] Tonson and Congreve did not abandon the capital, however; they simply learned to modulate it.

The distance between the 1710 edition of Congreve's works and the early collected editions of Pope is fairly short — only seven years — and David Foxon has demonstrated, at great length and in painstaking detail, the care with which Pope revised the accidentals of his work "at least as thoroughly as he revised the words of his text."[12] Pope's pioneering abandonment of capitals began in his collected *Works* of 1717 and was continued in his miscellaneous *Poems on Several Occasions*, where he imposed this new convention on his fellow contributors. Proof-sheets for the first two volumes of Pope's *Iliad* unmistakably show us, moreover, that it was the poet rather than his printer, William Bowyer, who was responsible for this usage, for we not only have the evidence of Pope's own hand on the proof-sheets but the testimony of Bowyer's other publications of this period, which all follow the traditional style. By the time the *Dunciad Variorum* was published in 1729, Pope had begun to abandon the use of italic type as well, and the so-called "death-bed" editions of 1743-44 show the entire range of his editorial activity: "first the abandonment of profuse italic, then of

initial capitals for common nouns, and finally the abandonment of italic for proper nouns."[13] Only John Gay, in Foxon's
view, was as bold a typographical revolutionary during the first
half of the eighteenth century.

It is worthwhile rehearsing the example of Pope in some
detail because of the prominence and prestige of his published
work and because of the obvious care he devoted to the presentation of his poetry on the printed page. But Pope is interesting
for two other reasons as well. In the first place, we need to realize that, despite Pope's insistence on these pervasive changes in
typographical convention between 1717 and his death in 1744, he
never followed this system in his own manuscripts.[14] Pope's
holographs clearly show that he continued to write his poetry
— and even revise it in fair copies — according to the traditional conventions; only in his proof-sheets and the revised
copies of his early editions do we see him actively changing the
style of his accidentals. This suggests, among other things, not
only that his manuscripts should not automatically be drawn
upon as copy-text by modern editors, but that Pope, like writers later in the century, created his work in the old style even as
he realized that it would eventually be published in the new. Old
habits seem to die hard, even for inveterate innovators.

The second point worth emphasizing about Pope's practice
is the fact that, like Ben Jonson before him, he distinguished
between different editions or formats of his works. The evidence of most of his publications after 1717 indicates that he
wished to classicize or romanize his verse, even though this
practice was in direct conflict with his continuing temptation to
use italics to make a point or mark an antithesis. Foxon concludes, however, that Pope consciously decided to employ italics in his trade editions — whether they were original folio
publications of his poems or the collected works in octavo —

whereas he avoided italics as far as possible in the large formats intended for a "select circle."[15] Perhaps Pope felt, Foxon speculates, "that the vulgar needed help in reading his work correctly, or at least that they should have italics for proper names as they would expect; and if these italics, why not others?"[16]

Given the powerful force of Pope's example, it might seem both natural and inevitable that English publications would move in the direction of Bronson's "Great Divide" sometime around 1750. My own research indicates, however, that this transformation did not take place as quickly, consistently, or completely as we might be led to believe. We need to consider, in the first place, the unusual nature of Pope's role. Pope was a shrewd businessman and a master manipulator as well as a painstaking writer and editor. His influence over Bowyer and his later printer, John Wright, was extraordinary, and it should not be assumed that many other writers of the time could lay claim to equal control of the printed word, although there are interesting exceptions such as Jonathan Richardson.[17] Printing conventions, including the presentation of capitals and italics, firmly fell within the purview of the trade during this period — compositors, correctors, printers, and booksellers — and the power of the booksellers in particular only increased during the middle years of the century.[18]

Pope was also, primarily, a poet; and poetry, important as it was, represented a relatively small percentage of the output of the London press during this period.[19] The English reader was assaulted by an astonishing array of literary genres ranging from sermons and histories to plays, political tracts, reference books, and the suddenly emerging novel of the 1740s. Many booksellers and printers specialized in a narrow spectrum of work, and there is no reason to believe that they would be unduly influenced by the rarified world of Augustan verse. And there was also, as Foxon's speculation about popular and refined editions suggests, significant variety within the reading public itself. If Pope himself sensed a need for retaining italicized pointing within the trade editions of his own poetry — which would presumably fall into the hands of most of his readers — we can begin to gauge how sophisticated indeed the members of his more select circle probably were. Pope's innovations, in other words, were not directed at his entire reading public, let alone at those readers whose normal choice of text was the ballad, broadside, newspaper, or chapbook.

My preliminary research indicates that this general transformation of printing conventions took much longer to complete than Bronson had realized or the revelations of Foxon's study of Pope might suggest. It is even difficult to define the word "complete," given the fact that English books are filled with inconsistency and exceptions throughout the century. At what point do we decide that such a change is statistically persuasive? And what do we make of the fact that a change in one convention — the abandonment of capitals for all substantive nouns, for example — could trigger a countervailing change in the opposite direction: the italicization of place names, for instance, or the placement of personified words in small caps? For an example of this modulation, we need look no further than the opening lines of Collins's *Oriental Eclogues*, where the italicized "*Selim*" of the 1742 edition now appears as "Selim"; only "sacred Truth" retains its original appearance.

The sheer number of books published at mid-century is daunting, moreover, and my observations in this essay are based on an examination of a thousand books, far from the entire complement of books published in London between 1740 and 1760, which the Eighteenth-Century Short-Title Catalog estimates to be 33,000.[20] The books I have examined suggest to me that this transformation was not pervasive, let alone complete, by the close of the 1750s. My research indicates that a majority of books did not appear in the new style until 1765, a full fifteen years after Bronson's "Great Divide." The sheer amount of inconsistency is also perplexing, especially when it occurs in the collaborative work of a single writer and book-seller, or even between the prefatory matter and the main text of the same book.

Certain patterns *are* clear, however, and I want to present two firm conclusions as well as one tentative one. My tentative claim is that sermons and other religious publications were just as likely as poetical texts to appear without the capitalization of common nouns in the 1740s. A handful of books published by Joseph Burroughs and Samuel Chandler in 1743, for instance, disclose remarkably modern texts, with italics used for biblical quotations and titles — and occasional emphasis — and with capitalization disappearing to the point where even the word "christianity" appears without an initial capital in Burroughs's *Defence of Two Discourses.*[21]

I find this to be an especially interesting development, for while the italic still reflects its historical role as "the typeface of privilege, as the type of quotation, of accuracy, obtrusion, asser-tion" (as Joseph Loewenstein has forcefully characterized it),[22] hierarchical distinctions involving the complex play among capitals, small caps, italic, and lower-case letters have signifi-cantly disappeared. "God" and "Christ" continue to be enshrined in capitals or small caps, but the rest of creation appears in a much more uniform style, with the result that the visual distinction between the divine and the human or secular is more pronounced than it formerly was. What I have not yet been able to determine is whether the publication of sermons and religious tracts followed denominational lines. John and

Charles Wesley, for instance, were continually publishing during this period, and the printing history of the Methodists needs to be traced with these changes in convention in mind.

My second conclusion is much firmer. In addition to examining individual publications as they appeared in the 1740s and 50s, it is also important to look carefully at the periodical press. The *Gentleman's Magazine*, founded by Edward Cave in 1731, provides a month-by-month digest of information and previously published material throughout this period, and I have found it particularly instructive to follow the fortunes of Cave's monthly installment of "Poetical Essays." The poetry Cave published in 1731 and 1732 vacillates between the old style and the new in the treatment of both capitals and italics. There is a revealing episode in January 1732, for instance, when Cave publishes the text of Colley Cibber's "Ode for New-Year's-Day 1732" with scant capitalization and a matching parody in the old style directly next to it on the same page, with the capitals and italics carefully employed to mark parodic difference (figure 21).

In 1733, however, matters begin to change abruptly. The January issue employs the new style, February reverts mostly to the old, March includes both, April returns almost completely to the old — and then, in May 1733, the "Poetical Essays" appear entirely in the new style. There is one exception to this development in June and one in July (perhaps because the poems were already in standing type), but none in August or September, and this virtual abandonment of capitals for common substantives holds throughout the ensuing months and years. Capitalized personifications and poems printed entirely in italic continue to appear in these monthly installments (perhaps to include more text, perhaps for the sake of visual variety), but a decisive change has clearly taken place. It is worth noting that this development occurs long before mid-

580   Poetical ESSAYS in JANUARY, 1732.   No. XIII.

O D E for New-Years-Day 1732. By C. Cibber, Efq; Poet Laureat.

The Poet Laureat's Ode for New-Years-Day burlefqu'd.

Recit.

A WAKE with joyous fongs the day
   That leads the op'ning year;
The year advancing to prolong,
Augustus' fway demands our fong,
And calls for univerfal cheer.

Air.

Your antient Annals, Britain, read,
   And mark the Reign you moft admire;
The prefent fhall the paft exceed,
   And yield enjoyment to defire.
Or if you find the coming year
In bleffings fhould tranfcend the laft
The diff'rence only will declare
The prefent fweeter than the paft.

Recit.

But, ah! the fweets his fway beftows,
Are greater far than Greatnefs knows.
With various penfive cares opprefs'd,
Unfeen, alas, the Royal Breaft
Endures his many a weight,
Unfelt by fwains of humble ftate.

Air.

Thus brooding on her lonely neft,
   Aloft the Eagle wakes,
   Her due delights forfakes,
Tho' Monarch of the air confefs'd,
Her drooping eyes refufe to clofe;
   While fearlefs of annoy,
   Her young belov'd enjoy
Protection, food, and fweet repofe.

Recit.

What thanks, ye Britons, can repay
So mild, fo juft, fo tender fway?

Air.

Your annual aid when he defires,
Lefs the King than land requires;
All the dues to him that flow
Are ftill but Royal wants to you:
So the feafons lend the earth
Their kindly rains to raife her birth,
And well the mutual labours fuit,
His the glory, yours the fruit.

Recit.

Affift, affift, ye fplendid throng,
Who now the Royal circle form;
With duteous wifhes blend the fong,
And every grateful wifh be warm.

C H O R V S.

May Cafar's health his reign fupply,
'Till faction fhall be pleas'd, or die;
'Till loyal hearts defire his fate:
   'Till happier fubjects know,
   Or foreign realms can fhow
A land fo blefs'd, a King fo great!
N. B. The Words and Expreffions in this Character being chiefly carp'd at, are defended by way of Irony in the Grub-ftreet Journal No. 105.]

Recit.

A Wake, with Grub-ftreet Odes, the Day
   That leads the op'ning Year;
The Year advancing to prolong
Great C--bb--r's Fame, demands a Song,
Infpir'd by Gin, or by Small Beer.

Air.

Your Ancient Ballad-Makers read,
   And mark the Fool you moft admire;
The prefent fhall the paft exceed,
   And yield Enjoyment to Defire:
Or, if you find the coming Ode,
In Nonfenfe fhould tranfcend the laft,
The Diff'rence only will make good
The prefent duller than the paft!

Recit.

But ah! the Stuff his Strain beftows
Is duller far than Dulnefs knows;
With various lumpifh Loads opprefft
Unfeen, alas! the Laureat's Breaft
Endures his many a Weight,
Unfelt by all but Bards of State.

Air.

Thus brooding o'er her lovely Neft,
   The watchful Owl awakes,
   Her due Delight forfakes,
Reftlefs to give all others Reft;
Her drooping Eyes refufe to clofe,
   Whilft, fearlefs of Numbers
   To threaten their Slumbers,
All around her enjoy much Sleep and Repofe.

Recit.

What Praifes can repay an Owl
So flat, fo heavy, and fo dull?
His annual Odes which he admires,
Lefs the Dunce than Fool infpires!
All the Strains which from him flow]
Are ftill of noble Ufe to you,
Whilft his kindly Sheets enrich
Every Bard to wipe his B——
And well the mutual Labours fuit,
His the Glory, yours the Fruit.

Recit.

Affift, affift, ye warbling Throng,
Who now the Grub-ftreet Chorus form;
With gen'rous Wifhes blend the Song,
And ev'ry grateful Wifh be warm.

C H O R V S,

May C--bb--r's Mufe his Odes fupply,
Till Nonfenfe fhall be pleas'd to die;
Till ftupid Fools defire hisPlace;
   Till happier Courts fhall know,
   Or Foreign Realms can fhow,
A Dunce fo dull, an Ode fo low;
What Thanks are due to —— s G——!

FIGURE 21.
Colley Cibber, "Ode for New-Year's-Day 1732," *Gentleman's Magazine* (1732).
By permission of the Boston Athenæum.

century and that the rest of each issue in 1733 — and long afterward — appears as thoroughly unrehabilitated prose, with every form of distinction imaginable cramming its already crowded columns. Only eleven years later, in his October 1744 issue, would Cave extend this ban on capitalized substantives to the extensive sections of prose in his magazine.

This emphasis on uniformity in the periodical press is similar, moreover, to the third pattern I have discovered, which is that this new house style was likely to be adopted when writers, editors, and booksellers issued collections of works written by diverse hands and previously published in diverse styles. This is true of the *Gentleman's Magazine* as early as 1733 and it continues all the way to Johnson's *Dictionary* in 1755, with its 116,000 illustrative quotations.[23] The publishing history of Robert Dodsley, however, provides the most interesting example.

Dodsley made a name for himself not just as a shrewd and successful bookseller ("Doddy, you know, is my patron," Johnson told Bennet Langton)[24] but also as an editor and writer. During the 1730s and 1740s, Dodsley's publications almost invariably appeared in the old style; because he employed different printers and was not always his own publisher, it seems reasonable to conclude that he preferred the traditional conventions to the new. By 1757, when he wrote to John Baskerville about the printer's new type specimens ("Your small letter is extreamly beautiful"), we sense a softening of attitude as he chides Baskerville for using "too many Capitals, which is generally thought to spoil the beauty of printing: but they should never be us'd to adjective verbs or adverbs."[25] But as late as 1761 we find the poet William Shenstone writing that "Spence, Burke, Lowth, and Melmoth, advise [Dodsley] to discard *Italicks*. I confess he has used them to a very great excess, but yet I do not think they should be utterly discarded."[26] Earlier, in 1744, we discover him publishing Mark Akenside's *Epistle to Curio* in the old style and Akenside's *Pleasures of Imagination* in the new, possibly (Foxon speculates) because Dodsley had shown the unknown Akenside's poem to Pope, who may — in approving it — have suggested how it might best be printed.[27]

In 1744, on the other hand, Dodsley also published his *Select Collection of Old Plays* in twelve volumes. This was an ambitious work of scholarship in which Dodsley made the texts of several old English plays available to the eighteenth-century reader for the first time. "I am, as it were," he wrote in his extensive preface to the first volume, "the first Adventurer on these Discoveries."[28] The preface itself is entirely printed in the old style, whereas the dramatic texts that follow are consistently printed in the new, with the traditional authorial voice thus quickly giving way to the new editorial style. Why should this be so? The answer lies in the nature of the material to be edited, which originally appeared in "so many Stiles and Manners of Writing" that Dodsley found he had to impose some form of uniformity on behalf of his contemporary readers.[29] At the same time, he was eager to show "the Progress and Improvement of our Taste and Language," and he therefore decided to retain the "very original Orthography" of the oldest plays whenever he had recourse to "first Editions."[30] The plays that appear in the first volume retain their old-spelling texts, which Dodsley believed would be "entertaining to the Curious." But he also realized that such a practice would be "very disagreeable" to "the Generality of Readers" and therefore attempted "to make the Reading as easy as I could in the rest" of the collection by modernizing the spelling and "privately" (silently) correcting or emending both substantives and punctuation.[31]

At no point in his preface does Dodsley address the issue of typographical style, but it is clear from his discussion of these other editorial issues that the imposition of this new style went hand in hand with his other efforts to modernize what appeared to him to be very unorthodox texts. Even the plays published with their original orthography, moreover, were printed without the traditional capitalization and use of italic. "The Pointing," he remarked in his preface, "is at the same time so preposterous (which, like false Guiding-Posts, are perpetually turning out of the High Road of Common Sense) that one would almost suspect there was as much Malice as Stupidity in these old Editions."[32] These words are suitably printed in the old style, with each substantive capitalized — a style of printing that was already appearing to many of his contemporaries as a preposterous practice, replete with false guiding-posts and departing from what we might now call the low road of common sense.

Robert Dodsley continued to publish his own work in the old style following the appearance of his *Select Collection of Old Plays* in 1744, but he returned to the new typographical conventions when he edited his influential *Collection of Poems* in 1748, 1753, and 1758 and his popular edition of *Select Fables*, printed by the now lean and spare Baskerville, in 1761.[33] When new English poems and old English plays officially entered the canon in the mid-decades of the century, they therefore did so in the new, uniform, crisper style that we continue to find in our anthologies today. Canonization and modernization went hand in hand.[34] And it is therefore also safe to conclude that editors had more influence on the evolution of the new style than writers did, even those as powerful as Pope. It was Dodsley as editor — rather than author or bookseller — who was responsible for these changes, or (and this is an important distinction) it was Dodsley as editor responding to the advice of his printers as well as his authors.

It is very difficult, finally, to adjudicate the relative importance of printers and booksellers in the slow evolution of style
toward the Great Divide. It is rare, for one thing, for printers to
be identified on the title-pages of books published during this
period, although there are often other sources for establishing
their roles. In his *Printer's Grammar* of 1755, James Smith noted
that "before we actually begin to compose, we should be
informed, either by the Author, or Master, after what manner
our work is to be done; whether the old way, with Capitals to
Substantives, and Italic to proper names; or after the more neat
practice, all in Roman, and Capitals to Proper names, and
Emphatical words."[35] (In his *Dictionary*, by the way, Johnson
defined "neat" as "Pure; unadulterated; unmingled.") Smith's
commentary indicates that the distinction between the old
manner and the new was quite clear, that a firm choice needed
to be made, that the choice did not (normally) lie in the hands
of the compositor, and that this question was still lingering as
late as 1755. Foxon argues, moreover, that printers themselves
did not have a house style which they imposed on their authors:
whatever uniformity there was in the eighteenth century, "the
burden must have fallen largely on the reader or corrector of the
press"[36] (a judgment that is largely corroborated by Smith).[37]

Was a change as fundamental as this — a change so dramatic and irreversible that it has permanently transformed
the look and texture of modern print culture in English —
actually determined by the individual or collective decisions
of countless and equally nameless eighteenth-century correctors? If so, then the denizens of the Augustan printing house
must have been aware of the concerns expressed, in print, over
the decisions they were taking, and they must have been
equally aware that the size and nature of their reading audience were changing as well.

III

There are a number of interesting signposts along the way. In Guy Miege's *English Grammar* of 1688, for instance, italic is proposed for frequent emphasis "as if the Reader had not sense to apprehend it, without so visible and palpable a distinction,"[38] a practice (as we have seen) that Pope retained in the trade editions of his poems. Similarly, in John Jones's *Practical Phonography* of 1701, we are told that printers generally place capital letters at the beginning of the common names of things, a practice that "daily gains ground."[39] Six years later Thomas Dyche, in his *Guide to the English Tongue*, reports that capitals are given to any substantive "if it bear any considerable stress of the Author's Sense upon it, to make it the more Remarkable and Conspicuous." But he then adds, in a footnote, that the custom of printing every substantive with an initial capital letter is "unnecessary, and hinders that remarkable Distinction intended by the Capitals."[40]

This is where Ephraim Chambers took up the argument in his much reprinted *Cyclopaedia* of 1728. Under his entry for capital letters, he wrote that "The *English* Printers have carried *Capitals* to a pitch of Extravagance; making it a Rule, to begin almost every Substantive with a *Capital*; which is a manifest Perversion of the Design of *Capitals*, as well as an Offence against Beauty and Distinctness." "Some of 'em," he adds, "begin now to retrench their superfluous *Capitals*, and to fall into the Measures of the Printers of other Nations" (1:154), but not in Chambers's own case, ironically, for his entire diatribe is printed in the old style, with a superfluity of capitals and italic alike. In the second edition of 1738, however, the capitalization disappears with the exception of the word "Capitals" itself, which remains true to its function until it is finally beheaded in the seventh edition of 1752.

It is significant that this debate involved not just writers and printers but grammarians and encyclopedists as well, for what is at stake here is not just the "proper" function of various typographical conventions but the necessity of employing these mediating modes of pointing, distinction, and emphasis in the first place. Chambers's hostility to the old way of doing things was based on "Extravagance," perversion of the proper role of capitals, and the abrogation of both beauty and consistency ("Distinctness"), which is another way of arguing that the very conventions which had been cultivated to provide the reader with helpful signposts had become impediments themselves to the comprehension of English poetry and prose.

Such a transformation in thinking about the nature of the conventions, moreover, presupposes a similar transformation in the sophistication of the reading public during the first half of the eighteenth century. And here, of course, we are on notoriously uncertain ground, for the various assessments of literacy, the reading public, and the sale and dissemination of newspapers, magazines, and books in the eighteenth century continue to differ from — if not actually contradict — one another. We have only to compare Samuel Johnson's description of "a nation of readers" in 1781 with his friend Edmund Burke's estimate, ten years later, that the English reading public included only 80,000 persons, less than ten percent of the entire population.[41] In his recent survey of the growth and nature of literacy, John Brewer cautions us that the most reliable figures are not very reliable at all, especially given the traditional definition of literacy as the ability to write one's name. He estimates that sixty percent of men and forty percent of women could read at mid-century, although these figures are significantly higher for the inhabitants of London, where female literacy seems to have reached sixty-six percent by the 1720s. These figures may have declined, however, late in the century.[42]

Brewer argues that "the growth in the reading public after 1700 would not have been possible without the gradual spread of literacy" and that without "readers the spurt in publishing that began in the late seventeenth century would have been impossible." But he nevertheless concludes that the major transformation that occurred was the change in the supply of printed matter following the removal of constraints imposed by the government and conservative booksellers alike. Such an increase in the amount of printed material "changed the nature of reading itself," he argues, particularly in the transition from "intensive" to "extensive" reading: from the careful perusal and re-reading of a few essential and relatively expensive volumes to the more exploratory and occasionally cursory examination of a wide variety of texts, including those that were ephemeral.[43] Brewer concludes that "Books, print and readers were everywhere. Not everyone was a reader, but even those who could not read lived to an unprecedented degree in a culture of print."[44]

Each of these factors — the rise in literacy and thus in the size of the reading public, the growth in publishing, the increasing variety of the publications themselves, and the changing nature of reading habits — directly bears on the evolution of the printed page. Type design, Stanley Morison once wrote, "moves at the pace of the most conservative reader,"[45] and much the same can be said of typographical conventions. When Pope stipulated that his works should appear in both popular and elite editions, he was counting on a sophisticated readership that could afford the higher cost of his classicized texts; but he was also acknowledging the fact that the general reading public still needed the typographical pointing to be found in the octavos and duodecimos. England may have been a nation of readers in 1781, but it was clearly a nation of different *kinds* of readers during the first half of the century.

Cautions concerning the nature of this larger reading public were voiced outside the confines of Pope's dunciadic vision as well as within it. Complaining in 1711 about the unfortunate desire of English poets and readers alike for "extremely *Gothick*" taste, Addison drew on Dryden's invidious distinctions, particularly his contempt of "the Rabble of Readers," "Mob-Readers," those who inhabit the "lowest Form" of the reading public for poetry.[46] In another issue of *The Spectator* Addison playfully referred to his "Illiterate Readers, if any such there are," as he boasted of the increase of learning in England and the consequent improvement in the art of printing.[47] As late as 1756, in the abridgment of his *Dictionary of the English Language,* Johnson could matter-of-factly recommend his pared-down volumes to "the greater number of readers, who, seldom intending to write or presuming to judge, turn over books only to amuse their leisure, and to gain degrees of knowledge suitable to lower characters, or necessary to the common business of life: these know not any other use of a dictionary than that of adjusting orthography, or explaining terms of science or words of infrequent occurrence, or remote derivation."[48] Being able to read, as Ian Watt pointed out decades ago in *The Rise of the Novel,* "was a necessary accomplishment only for those destined to the middle-class occupations — commerce, administration and the professions"; only "a small proportion of the labouring classes who were technically literate developed into active members of the reading public, and . . . the majority of these were concentrated in those employments where reading and writing" were vocational necessities.[49]

The distinctions that continued to be made among English

readers of the first half of the century thus provide another crucial context in which to place this gradual but steady change in
printing history. It is one thing to associate the abandonment of
capitals and italics with the growth of literacy, the reading public, and print culture; it is another, however, to place it within a
rapidly evolving society in which the relative sophistication of
readers was still an issue. The printing practices of the 1740s and
1750s suggest to me that, individually and perhaps even collec-
tively, writers, compositors, correctors, printers, booksellers,
and readers agreed that the reading population as a whole could
accommodate these new typographical conventions and the
change in taste they represented. Year by year, printer by printer,
publication by publication, the printed material of mid-eighteenth-century England appeared in a less hierarchical, less differentiated, less heavily textured style.

This pervasive leveling of the text, with its less visually and
intellectually mediated form of presentation, in turn placed
much more emphasis on the discriminating power of the individual reader. These fundamental changes in printing conventions, in other words, are not only a result (and reflection) of the
development of the reading public, but also a cause of increased
facility and sophistication as readers were faced with a greater
uniformity in the presentation of printed texts. Such a revolutionary development did not go unnoticed, of course, and the
most vociferous opposition to these changes was voiced —
much too late in the century, as it turned out — by Benjamin
Franklin. Writing to his son William in 1773, Franklin complained about the reprinting of one of his anonymous pieces,
which had been "stripped of all the capitalling and italicing, that
intimate the allusions and marks the emphasis of written discourses, to bring them as near as possible to those spoken."
Printing such a piece "in one even small character," he added,

"seems to me like repeating one of Whitefield's sermons in the monotony of a school-boy."[50] Later still, in a famous letter to Noah Webster of 1789, Franklin repeated his concern about the difficulty of reading modern texts aloud, noting that "the Eye generally slides forward three or four Words before the Voice" and therefore relies upon distinctions within the visual field in order to modulate one's expression.[51]

But Franklin's principal concern is with the sheer difficulty of understanding a less visually differentiated text. In examining books published between the Restoration in 1660 and the accession of George II in 1727, he observes that "all *Substantives* were begun with a capital, in which we imitated our Mother Tongue, the German," a practice that was particularly helpful to those who were not well acquainted with English and its "prodigious Number" of words that are both verbs and substantives. Franklin (and who would know better?) ascribes this change to "the Fancy of Printers," who believe that the suppression of capitals "shows the Character to greater Advantage; those Letters prominent above the line disturbing its even regular Appearance." The "Effect of this Change is so considerable," he writes, that a learned Frenchman who used to read English books with some ease now found them difficult to understand, blaming the stylistic obscurity of modern English writers because he did not realize that the printing conventions themselves had changed.[52]

I V

By 1789, of course, Franklin was espousing a lost cause. The look of the English page had thoroughly evolved into the form with which we are familiar today — even to the point of tending to drop the traditional long "s" and the ligatures in which it was embedded (another of Franklin's concerns).[53] The fact that these changes intensified at mid-century, moreover, suggests to me that cultural forces were at work which extended far beyond the growth of the reading public or the sophistication of the individual reader. The phenomenon I have been mapping is, by its very nature, an amorphous one, appearing not at a single, distinct moment but in tens of thousands of books over a period of several decades. It is therefore useful to associate these changes with other, more discrete phenomena, keeping in mind Foucault's proviso that such changes did not necessarily "occur at the same level, proceed at the same pace, or obey the same laws."[54]

What I specifically have in mind is the desire at mid-century for the rationalization of knowledge and of the formal means by which it is represented. We find this strongly emerging tendency in everything from what Lawrence Lipking has characterized as "the ordering of the arts" in eighteenth-century England to the publication, in the late 1760s, of Blackstone's *Commentaries*.[55] As Paul Langford has argued, Blackstone's pioneering volumes were designed "to explain the arcane mysteries of English law to an audience which had the intelligence and interest to grasp its principles, but was too busy serving the diverse requirements of a complex, developing society to put itself through the costly experience of a traditional legal education." And "practically every learned and scientific specialism," Langford adds, "had its Blackstone in the middle of the eighteenth century, appealing to much the same readership."[56]

At the heart of these developments was an attempt to codify knowledge and, in so doing, to impose some degree of uniformity on conventions that were widely believed to be inconsistent, capricious, and irregular — not to mention out of step with England's neighbors on the continent. Johnson's great *Dic-*

tionary, published in 1755 and seven years in the making, represents an ambitious and complicated attempt to achieve both of these goals. The "one great end of this undertaking," Johnson wrote in his *Plan* of 1747 (published by Dodsley and his associates in the new style, by the way), "is to fix the English language," an undertaking that he eventually realized would be impossible.[57] Our language, he opined, "now stands in our dictionaries a confused heap of words, without dependence, and without relation."[58] The chief rule he proposed to follow, however, was "to make no innovation, without a reason sufficient to balance the inconvenience of change," for "All change is of itself an evil," he wrote in the *Plan*.[59] But systematic attempts were nevertheless needed to impose coherence on an idiom "composed of dissimilar parts, thrown together by negligence, by affectation, by learning, or by ignorance."[60] Orthography, pronunciation, etymology, and definitions all had to be established, and Johnson's groundbreaking (and backbreaking) innovation was to balance his own judgment against the collective authority of the best English writers, particularly those before the Restoration, whose works he regarded, as he remarked in his "Preface," as "*the wells of English undefiled*" (a phrase printed in italics, by the way, to indicate that it is a quotation).[61]

The "Preface" of 1755 and the dictionary that follows it in two folio volumes reveal the extent to which Johnson was forced to back away from his intention to "fix" the English language, relenting in the face of what he called "the boundless chaos of a living speech."[62] Etymology gave way to usage and uniformity to custom; staunchly held beliefs concerning the evils of change were tempered, in the "Preface," into commendations of "constancy and stability," in which one finds a "general and lasting advantage."[63] "I am not yet so lost in lexicography," he wrote, "as to forget that *words are the daugh-*

ters of earth, and that things are the sons of heaven" (also suitably printed in italics, by the way).[64] Language is only the instrument of science, and yet Johnson could still wish that the instrument itself "might be less apt to decay."[65]

At the close of his *Plan*, Johnson confessed that the extent of the project he had so ambitiously surveyed made him feel like Caesar's soldiers, gazing at a "new world, which it is almost madness to invade." Perhaps with Dodsley's introduction to his *Select Collection of Plays* of 1744 echoing in his ear, Johnson announced that, even if he did not complete the conquest, he should "at least discover the coast, civilize part of the inhabitants, and make it easy for some other adventurer to proceed farther, to reduce them wholly to subjection, and settle them under laws."[66] The opening pages of the "Preface" are much more muted, but Johnson's accomplishment is no less clear. The lexicographer found "our speech copious without order, and energetick without rules"; desperately needed were established principles of selection, settled tests of purity, and the suffrages of acknowledged authority.[67] And thus Johnson "accumulated in time the materials of a dictionary, which, by degrees, I reduced to method, establishing to myself, in the progress of the work, such rules as experience and analogy suggested to me."[68]

It was, famously, a solitary task completed by a single scholar in the space of seven years, whereas it had taken the forty French academicians forty years to complete their own *dictionnaire*. The counterexample of the French academy and their dictionary — and the great Italian *Vocabulario degli Accademici della Crusca* as well — remained deeply impressed on Johnson's mind as well as those of his contemporaries. We "have long preserved our constitution," he wrote in the "Preface"; "let us make some struggles for our language."[69] The making of the dictionary was, by definition (so to speak), a nationalistic undertaking, predicated on clearly articulated needs but simultaneously enshrining the most polished of English writers.

This complicated tension between what must be lamented and what can be celebrated is reinforced, moreover, by Johnson's ambivalence towards French culture and the elegance of its language. I have already drawn attention to how he remarks, in the "Preface," that "Our language, for almost a century, has, by the concurrence of many causes, been gradually departing from its original *Teutonick* character [spelled, by the way, with a "k"], and deviating towards a *Gallick* structure and phraseology, from which it ought to be our endeavour to recal it," primarily by "making our ancient volumes the groundwork of stile."[70] At the same time, it is manifestly the purpose of the *Dictionary* to supply for Great Britain what the French and Italians already enjoy. It may do so by canonizing what is most genuinely English — and by avoiding the undue contamination of continental drift — but the example and influence of European models cannot be entirely neglected. Johnson is forced, in the *Plan* of the *Dictionary*, to praise the accuracy of French and Italian pronunciation, which are now "fix'd," and to refer to them, at least in this context, as "more polished languages" than his native English.[71] Johnson's immense project will itself produce a more polished language, but it will do so by supplying the rules, judgment, rationalization, and authorities that are historically lacking.

V

Let me suggest one additional counter-example, no less complicated than the first. In 1752, while Johnson was deep in the process of preparing his *Dictionary*, he went to sleep on Wednesday, September 2nd, and woke the next morning on

Thursday the 14th. This long sleep was occasioned by an act of Parliament that enabled the British to move from the Old Style Julian calendar to the New Style Gregorian calendar, which had been adopted by Catholic countries in 1582-83 and by most Protestant countries around 1700. The English court had approved such a change as early as 1584, but the Protestant bishops were not eager to adopt a proposal from the Pope, and they replied to Sir Francis Walsingham's inquiries with delaying tactics that proved to be effective. By 1735, however, a proposed change was taken up in earnest in the press, and in 1751 an act of Parliament "for regulating the commencement of the year, and for correcting the calendar now in use" was successfully sponsored by the Earl of Macclesfield and by Lord Chesterfield — who served not only as one of the King's secretaries of state, but as the undisputed arbiter of polite behavior as well as the authority on polite linguistic usage to whom Johnson dexterously deferred in his *Plan* of the *Dictionary*.[72]

Although there was some opposition to the adoption of the Gregorian calendar, it was generally muted: the friction between Protestant and Catholic causes was less important, as Paul Alkon has shown, than "the desire to rationalize timekeeping systems for commercial purposes" as well as for public worship.[73] The only nationalistic rhetoric raised at the time was an appeal to patriotic shame at the way England had lagged behind other Protestant countries in taking such a "rational step." This change of calendar occurred, moreover, amid similar debates concerning the rationalization of English weights, measures, coinage, and even the introduction of a national census.[74] And this, it seems to me, is precisely the cultural environment in which printing conventions could also undergo a similar transformation from the old style to the new: in a nation comfortable with the prospect of change, ready to accept uniform standards and conventions, and confident enough to do so in a manner that would no longer place them out of step with most of the continent. Despite the Jacobite rising in 1745, the Seven Years' War that began in 1756, and a Hanoverian dynasty on the throne, the English were nonetheless willing to synchronize themselves in their calendars and on the printed page roughly at mid-century, high Georgian noon.

These analogies obviously have their limits. Johnson, after all, resisted the Gallic and embraced the Teutonic even as he strove to fix the language and codify its laws. Writers, including Johnson, continued to capitalize and italicize their substantives throughout the century, and Johnson continued to depart from his own orthography at every turn.[75] Like many of his contemporaries, Johnson followed the new-style calendar with its renumbering of the days of public worship, but reverted to the old style in commemorating personal events: his birthday on September 7th (which he observed on the 18th) or the death of his wife Tetty, which he also observed eleven days later.[76] It could be argued, moreover, that the old style of printing enjoyed its own codification and principles, and that what the new style offered in terms of evenness and regularity it lacked in precise linguistic differentiation. This was Franklin's essential objection to what he characterized as "Improvements *backwards*" ("Improvements" capitalized, by the way, "*backwards*" in italic).[77]

By the way? My parenthetical asides throughout this essay have a consistent point, of course, which is to register the intentionality of the printed or written act and the importance of this particular "bibliographical code."[78] No matter how complicated or amorphous these changes in printing conventions may turn out to be, they were anything but accidental, which Johnson defined as "Casual, fortuitous, happening by chance." The *presentation* of substantives directly affects — and may even control — the meaning as well as the texture of the printed word. When Johnson went on to define "accidental" as a noun — as a substantive — he referred to it as "A property nonessential" and quoted the following sentence from Isaac Watts's *Logick*: "Conceive, as much as you can, of the essentials of any subject, before you consider its *accidentals*." In this essay I have attempted to refute Johnson (as well as Greg) *thus*, considering the accidentals first in order to demonstrate the ways in which printing history reveals the general impress of cultural change while also working to generate it. As the American printer Daniel Berkeley Updike nicely put it, "we unconsciously govern our printing by the kind of life we approve."[79] The example of printing history in mid-eighteenth-century London suggests that Johnson's, Collins's, and Dodsley's contemporaries approved of a renewed emphasis on the discriminatory powers of the individual reader by means of what we, today, would characterize as a less cluttered, more elegant, more aesthetically polished text. It also suggests a willingness to accept, if perhaps not quite to embrace, an insistence on uniformity and regularity well beyond the confines of the printed page.

NOTES

Epigraph: Samuel Johnson, "Preface to the English Dictionary," in Johnson, *Poetry and Prose*, ed. Mona Wilson (London: Rupert Hart-Davis, 1950), p. 320.

1. Johnson, *Poetry and Prose*, p. 314.

2. *The Works of William Collins*, ed. Richard Wendorf and Charles Ryskamp (Oxford: Clarendon Press, 1979), p. 104.

3. W. W. Greg, "The Rationale of Copy-Text" (1950), in *Bibliography and Textual Criticism: English and American Literature 1700 to the Present*, ed. OM Brack Jr. and Warner Barnes (Chicago: Univ. of Chicago Press, 1969), p. 43: "We need to draw a distinction between the significant, or as I shall call them 'substantive,' readings of the text, those namely that affect the author's meaning or the essence of his expression, and others, such in general as spelling, punctuation, word-division, and the like, affecting mainly its formal presentation, which may be regarded as the accidents, or as I shall call them 'accidentals,' of the text." The argument of my essay, on the other hand, is that "formal presentation" directly affects the author's meaning and expression, although it should be kept in mind that Greg himself was empirical rather than prescriptive in his views. For similar arguments to mine on behalf of the role of accidentals, see especially D. F. McKenzie, *Bibliography and the Sociology of Texts* (1986; rev. edn., Cambridge: Cambridge Univ. Press, 1999), and Jerome J. McGann, *A Critique of Modern Textual Criticism* (1983; rpt. Charlottesville and London: Univ. Press of Virginia, 1992).

4. Bertrand Harris Bronson, "Printing as an Index of Taste," in *Facets of the Enlightenment: Studies in English Literature and Its Contexts* (Berkeley and Los Angeles: Univ. of California Press, 1968), pp. 339-340.

5. Ibid., p. 340.

6. David Foxon, "Poets and Compositors," unpublished sixth Lyell lecture, pp. 228-229. Copies of this lecture are deposited in several major libraries, including the British Library. I am grateful to David L. Vander Muelen for providing me with a copy and thereby drawing my attention to this text, which is in many ways a rough draft whose quotations and conclusions need to be verified.

7. Ibid., pp. 238-240.

8. Ibid., p. 235.

9. D. F. McKenzie, "Typography and Meaning: The Case of William Congreve," in *Buch und Buchhandel in Europa im achtzehnten*

Jahrhundert / The Book and the Book Trade in Eighteenth-Century Europe, ed. Giles Barber and Bernhard Fabian, Proceedings of the Fifth Wolfenbütteler Symposium (Hamburg: Ernst Hauswedell, 1977), p. 110.

10. Ibid., p. 117.

11. Ibid., p. 116.

12. David Foxon, *Pope and the Early Eighteenth-Century Book Trade*, rev. and ed. James McLaverty (Oxford: Clarendon Press, 1991), p. 153.

13. Ibid., p. 179.

14. Ibid., p. 186 and passim.

15. Ibid., p. 196.

16. Ibid., p. 196.

17. See, for instance, Richard Wendorf, *The Elements of Life: Biography and Portrait-Painting in Stuart and Georgian England* (Oxford: Clarendon Press, 1990), pp. 136-150.

18. For the relative autonomy of the printer, see Philip Gaskell, *A New Introduction to Bibliography* (New York and Oxford: Oxford Univ. Press, 1972), pp. 40-43 and 339 (where n. 6 refers to changes in printing practices in the mid-eighteenth century). For a discussion of the book trade, see Terry Belanger, "Publishers and writers in eighteenth-century England," in *Books and their Readers in Eighteenth-Century England*, ed. Isabel Rivers (Leicester: Leicester Univ. Press; New York: St. Martin's Press, 1982), pp. 5-25, and John Brewer, *The Pleasures of the Imagination: English Culture in the Eighteenth Century* (London: HarperCollins; New York: Norton, 1997), p. 477.

19. John Feather, "British Publishing in the Eighteenth Century: a preliminary subject analysis," *The Library* 6th ser., 8 (1986): 32-46, shows that literature represented about 20% of all titles and that poetry represented 47% of all literary titles.

20. This figure does not include periodicals or later editions of books printed earlier. The *total* figure for all such imprints between 1740 and

1760 is approximately 52,500. I am grateful to John Bloomberg-Rissman of the ESTC for this information.

21. Published by John Noon, *A Defence of Two Discourses* begins entirely in the new style; caps are used for the occasional important word, such as "Truth" or "Saviour"; italics are used for Biblical quotations, for titles, and for emphasis. For the most part, however, this is a book with very modest capitalization.

22. Joseph F. Loewenstein, "*Idem*: italics and the genetics of authorship," *Journal of Medieval and Renaissance Studies* 20:2 (Fall 1990): 224.

23. This figure is drawn from Lawrence Lipking, *Samuel Johnson: The Life of an Author* (Cambridge: Harvard Univ. Press, 1998), p. 117.

24. James Boswell, *Boswell's Life of Johnson*, ed. George Birkbeck Hill, rev. L. F. Powell (Oxford: Clarendon Press, 1934-50), 1:326.

25. *The Correspondence of Robert Dodsley 1733-1764*, ed. James E. Tierney (Cambridge: Cambridge Univ. Press, 1988), p. 273.

26. Ralph Straus, *Robert Dodsley* (London: John Lane, 1910), p. 291.

27. Foxon, "Poets and Compositors," p. 256.

28. Robert Dodsley, ed., *A Select Collection of Old Plays* (London, 1744), 1:xxxv.

29. Ibid., 1:xxxxvii.

30. Ibid., 1:xxxvi.

31. Ibid., 1:xxxvi.

32. Ibid., 1:xxxxvii.

33. For a full discussion of Dodsley's editorial roles, affecting both substantives and accidents, see Richard Wendorf, "Dodsley as Editor," *Studies in Bibliography* 31 (1978): 235-248, rpt. as ch. 8 in this volume.

34. I am speaking here of eighteenth-century poetry in particular as it began to be anthologized and thereby placed within the "modern" canon. For a discussion of canon formation during this period that

focuses on the enshrinement of Spenser, Shakespeare, and Milton as the exemplars of the English literary tradition, see Jonathan Brody Kramnick, *Making the English Canon: Print-Capitalism and the Cultural Past, 1700-1770* (Cambridge: Cambridge Univ. Press, 1998), who essentially argues that the Augustans' early-eighteenth-century commodification of politeness and refinement in the canon (as represented by Waller, Denham, and even the modernization of Elizabethan texts) was replaced by a mid-eighteenth-century valuation of "an abstruse, quasi-Latinate vernacular in older, canonical English" and a concurrent disavowal of modern politeness and the novel (pp. 43-44). "The project of surmounting the difficulty and vulgarity of England's past gives way to one of appreciating the linguistic distance and aesthetic difficulty of Spenser, Shakespeare, and Milton" (p. 44).

The changes in typographical conventions that I have been charting in this essay would seem to dovetail with this first, early movement toward refinement and politeness, although it must be kept in mind that this "modernization" of capitals and italics posed difficulties for readers who were used to relying upon the distinctions and emphasis the older style conveyed. Presumably the conscious valuation of "the difficulty and vulgarity of England's past" at mid-century flies in the face of attempts like Dodsley's to rationalize and refine the texts of old English plays.

35. J. Smith, *The Printer's Grammar* (London, 1755), p. 201; elsewhere he refers to the old way as the "common" way (p. 168) and the new as "the more modern and neater way" (pp. 201-202).

36. Foxon, "Poets and Compositors," p. 244.

37. Smith, *The Printer's Grammar*, p. 199: following copy is a "good law . . . now looked upon as obsolete" because authors expect "the Printer to spell, point, and digest their Copy, that it may be intelligible to the Reader." The compositor and corrector have joint responsibility for this; both need a "liberal education" (p. 200). Correctors should revise copy before it goes to the compositor if they suspect any problems, including capitalization (p. 273). Correctors

are chosen from compositors "who are thought capable of that office" (p. 274-275).

38. Quoted by Foxon, *Pope and the Early Eighteenth-Century Book Trade*, pp. 180-181.

39. Ibid., pp. 181-182.

40. Ibid., p. 182.

41. For Johnson, see *Lives of the Poets*, ed. George Birkbeck Hill (Oxford: Clarendon Press, 1905), 3:19, cited by Ian Watt, *The Rise of the Novel: Studies in Defoe, Richardson and Fielding* (Berkeley and Los Angeles: Univ. of California Press, 1957), p. 37; for Burke, see Richard Altick, *The English Common Reader* (Chicago: Univ. of Chicago Press, 1950), p. 49. Both Watt and Altick take these statements with a large pinch of salt — and both of their pioneering books are still worth consulting. My own sense is that Johnson was referring to the palpable *growth* in reading of all kinds during the second half of the century as well as the rise of the "common reader," whereas Burke may have been drawing a distinction between the educated sector of the public and less sophisticated readers. Johnson would elsewhere refer, satirically, to "a nation of writers."

42. Brewer, *The Pleasures of the Imagination*, pp. 167-168.

43. Ibid., p. 169. The model distinguishing between intensive and extensive reading was developed by Rolf Engelsing, a German historian; see Robert DeMaria, Jr., "Samuel Johnson and the Reading Revolution," *Eighteenth-Century Life* 16 (1992): 86-102.

44. Brewer, *The Pleasures of the Imagination*, p. 187.

45. Quoted by Bronson, "Printing as an Index of Taste," p. 326.

46. *The Spectator*, ed. Donald F. Bond (Oxford: Clarendon Press, 1965), 1:269.

47. Ibid., 3:382. By "Illiterate Readers" Addison may also have been drawing on the traditional definition of literacy, in elite circles, as a knowledge of both Greek and Latin.

48. Samuel Johnson, *A Dictionary of the English Language*, abridged edition (1756), vol. 1, "Preface." See Allen Reddick, *The Making of Johnson's Dictionary 1746-1773* (Cambridge: Cambridge Univ. Press, 1990), pp. 86-87, for a discussion of this edition.

49. Watt, *The Rise of the Novel*, pp. 39-40.

50. Benjamin Franklin, *Writings*, ed. J. A. Leo Lemay (New York: Library of America, 1987), p. 886.

51. Ibid., p. 1177.

52. Ibid., p. 1176.

53. Ibid., p. 1177. The disappearance of the long "s" in England was greatly influenced by French practices according to James Mosley, "s & f: the origin and use of the 'long s'" (single sheet, various issues, 1993-99; rpt. in Steven Tuohy, *James Mosley: a checklist of the published writings 1958-95* [Over, Cambridgeshire: Rampant Lion Press, 1995], pp. 20-22). For the possible influence of Spanish printers, see Mosley's "The disuse of long s in Spain" (single sheet, London, 2000).

54. Michel Foucault, *The Order of Things: An Archaeology of the Human Sciences* (New York: Random House, 1970), p. xii.

55. Lawrence Lipking, *The Ordering of the Arts in Eighteenth-Century England* (Princeton: Princeton Univ. Press, 1970).

56. Paul Langford, *A Polite and Commercial People: England 1727-1783* (Oxford: Clarendon Press, 1989), p. 2.

57. Johnson, *Poetry and Prose*, p. 127.

58. Ibid., p. 128.

59. Ibid., p. 126.

60. Ibid., p. 130.

61. Ibid., p. 314.

62. Ibid., p. 307.

63. Ibid., p. 304.

64. Ibid., p. 304.

65. Ibid., p. 305.

66. Ibid., p. 138.

67. Ibid., p. 301.

68. Ibid., p. 302.

69. Ibid., p. 322.

70. Ibid., p. 314.

71. Ibid., p. 128.

72. My summary is indebted to E. G. Richards, *Mapping Time: The Calendar and its History* (Oxford: Oxford Univ. Press, 1998), pp. 247-256.

73. Paul Alkon, "Changing the Calendar," *Eighteenth-Century Life* 7:2 (Jan. 1982): 7. Alkon's work is corroborated and expanded by Robert Poole, *Time's alteration: Calendar reform in early modern England* (London: University College London Press, 1998).

74. See, for example, Julian Hoppit, "Reforming Britain's Weights and Measures, 1660-1824," *English Historical Review* 108 (1993): 82-104, and Peter Buck, "People who counted: Political arithmetic in the eighteenth century," *Isis* 73 (1982): 28-45.

Although I do not have space to draw an extended parallel in this essay, it should at least be noted here that the adoption of printing conventions at mid-century which were generally thought to be more elegant and refined can profitably be compared with a similar development in English prose itself. For a thorough analysis of changes in linguistic usage, see Carey McIntosh, *The Evolution of English Prose 1700-1800: Style, Politeness, and Print Culture* (Cambridge: Cambridge Univ. Press, 1998), who charts the movement toward a "standardization" that encourages "formality, precision, and abstractness in language," "a trend towards writtenness and away from the redundancy, sloppiness, and concreteness of speech" (pp. 23-24).

75. Foxon charts the consistency or inconsistency of authors' manu-

scripts versus their printed texts in "Poets and Compositors."

76. Samuel Johnson, *Diaries, Prayers, and Annals,* ed. E. L. McAdam, Jr., with Donald and Mary Hyde, The Yale Edition of the Works of Samuel Johnson, vol. 1 (New Haven: Yale Univ. Press; London: Oxford Univ. Press, 1958), pp. 3, 49, 50 (the anniversary of his wife's death), and 309 (his birthday).

77. Franklin, *Writings,* p. 1177.

78. D. C. Greetham, foreword to McGann's *Critique of Modern Textual Criticism,* p. xviii, where he contrasts the "bibliographical codes" of a text (typography, layout, paper, order) with "linguistic" ones (the words of the text).

79. Quoted by Bronson, "Printing as an Index of Taste," p. 326.

Index

This book has been set in the typeface *Minion*,
designed by Robert Slimbach and first
released by Adobe in 1990.

Designed by Scott Vile at the Ascensius Press,
South Freeport, Maine, and printed in an
edition of one thousand by
Sheridan Books.